MARY'S COLLEGE OF EDUCATION

PUT IT IN

Writing

Based on the *Sunday Times* Magazine series

J. M. Dent & Sons Ltd
London and Melbourne

First published 1984
© John Whale, 1984

Phototypeset in 11/14 pt Linotron Plantin Light by
Tradespools Ltd, Frome

Made in Great Britain by
Biddles Ltd, Guildford, Surrey for
J. M. Dent & Sons Ltd
Aldine House, 33 Welbeck Street, London W1M 8LX

British Library Cataloguing in Publication Data

Whale, John
  Put it in writing.
  1. English language—Rhetoric
  I. Title
  808   PE1408
ISBN 0-460-04582-2

CONTENTS

PREFACE

Habits of writing are as personal as toothbrushes. Giving advice about writing is an intrusive, sometimes an impertinent, exercise; people undertaking it do well to explain what has impelled them.

My first interest in written English was prompted by the sound of it, when my father, with a preacher's skill, read 19th-century classics—Scott, Dickens, Borrow, Kinglake, Trollope—aloud to his children. At wartime and postwar boarding-schools I had time to read a great deal besides. Since then, the accidents of journalistic employment have drawn me repeatedly into broadcasting; so that even when I write for print I cannot help listening to the way words sound.

For four autumns, between 1980 and 1983, I taught writing—in the interstices of my own journalistic work—to a handful of graduate students from the University of Missouri journalism school: they were being found room at my newspaper, the *Sunday Times*. At the same time my unofficial care for the paper's literacy (I had been on the staff since 1969) developed into a substantive duty. After a time it seemed to me that the lessons I learnt from both tasks might have a general usefulness as a sequence of published pieces.

I put the idea to the *Sunday Times* Magazine, which has carried many an instructional series on other topics: the suggestion was generously received by the editor, Peter Jackson, and his deputy, Philip Clarke, and a formula was evolved with them. A series of 30 half-page articles, each something under 700 words in length, appeared weekly in the magazine between September 1983 and April 1984. It is that series, augmented and indexed, that makes up this book.

Just as my long-standing interest in the sound of English gives the book a bias towards the notion of prose as a thing heard, not just a thing written down, so my recent work as teacher and critical reader gives the book a preoccupation with certain problems of writing in particular: those problems which working professional writers, or intending professionals, do in fact appear to overlook or find difficult. A book of this kind needs limits, and I have chosen those. A reader or a colleague has sometimes said, for example, 'Do a piece about "shall" and "will"'; and I have not risen to the suggestion, because I have not found that the problem is one which comes between my sample of writers and effective writing.

Still, I have been able to take in a good many of the suggestions made to me by those whom I must now (as a broadcaster again) call my former colleagues at the paper, and my former students from the United States, and my former readers in the magazine. I offer this little book gratefully to all of them, and to anyone else who may find it helpful.

I   SOUNDING LIKE YOURSELF

1
INTRODUCTORY

Virtually all the people who pick up this book are already writers. They may still be at the stage of setting out what they know about Morton's Fork or the Diet of Worms on one side of the paper only. They may have reached 'To the editor: Sir, My attention has been drawn . . .' At countless points along that line the written word is regularly wrung from them. They write letters, of affection or application or complaint; they write memos or instructions; they write reports for their club journal or their parish magazine or their local paper.

Some of them can do all those things well. They know what fits—what kind of words and phrases suit the context and their own character; and they know how to keep within established current usage. This understanding, general and detailed, allows them to keep their readers contentedly reading.

But there are a great many people whose touch is less certain than that. For one reason or another, the necessary understanding has in part eluded them. Many of them are aware of the problem themselves: they suspect that their sentences are too clumsy to represent them fairly, or that their way with commas or apostrophes or hyphens may put purist readers off.

This series is meant to put heart into those people, by reminding them that in their own speech, their own ear, their own sense of logic and their own reading they already command much of the equipment they need for effective writing.

Sceptics say that writing can't be taught: it's too private a process. They could certainly maintain that offering to teach it is a rash act. Yet something that can be taught is preparation: decent mastery of your material, orderly planning of how to set it out. Another thing that can be taught is revision. For the writer, the great virtue of the written word is that it's improvable. With the spoken word, the first version is usually also the last. Not so with writing. Before it leaves you, words can be moved or altered, sentences and paragraphs broken up or joined together, passages added or taken away, until they express meaning and emphasis and character as fitly as you can make them. A word-processor helps, say the converted, but you can make the changes perfectly well with paper and a ball-point pen. It's at the revision stage in particular that I hope this book will be helpful.

Most of all, a principle that can be taught is the principle of learning from good models. Many handbooks on the mechanics of writing teach deliberately from bad models. They hold up an inept sentence and laugh at it.

I doubt very much whether that is a useful method. It saps confidence. Instead of encouraging people to put themselves on paper in the words that most easily come to them, safe in the knowledge that they can tidy up afterwards, it fosters the belief that writing is immensely difficult—that the writer is like a burglar in a silver-vault, fated to set bells jangling as soon as he steps across any of a multitude of laser beams, and yet having very little idea where they are.

It suggests that good writing is a matter of right and wrong: some things are correct, others incorrect, and you should know which is which or hold your peace. In fact, though, a living language is both more subtle and more accommodating than that. Certainly there are customs it is wise to observe, if your meaning is to be plain and your readers are to stay happy. But these customs are not carved in marble: they are derived from nothing more imposing than the usage of good modern writers—which varies between and even within the work of different writers, and is constantly added to as new things are written.

That begs the question, I know, of who good modern writers

4

are. But it is a question you are at liberty to answer for yourself, in the light of your own present judgment and the context you are writing in. That is the measure of the latitude you have. You may find good writing—in tune with common speech, readily understood, neat, vivid—in something as humble as a road-sign (like that economical American warning 'BRIDGES FREEZE BEFORE HIGHWAYS'). I shall make suggestions about other sources; you will build your own list.

In the actual practice of writing, there are far fewer things that could fairly be called rules than is often supposed. A lot of people make life a burden for themselves, both as writers and readers, by imagining rules where there are none. I often encounter the belief, for example, that you must never have a comma before 'and' or 'but'. If a rule of writing has been constantly broken by good writers, it is no rule. In writing, as in religion, much harm is done by the assertion of certainties where none exist.

I believe that there is no way of learning to write so effective as observant reading; and that, given a few preliminary pointers, you can draw from your reading a handful of broad principles which will guide you both in general and in detail. These principles will help you write appropriately and attractively, and also help you avoid phrasing or punctuation which will obscure your meaning or break your reader's concentration.

So each chapter in this book will be a sermon on a text. Each chapter will start with a few sentences of what seems to me good writing, nearly always published since the Second World War. Then it will take a swift critical look at the way the writer meets the question I want to consider: how to plan, how to begin, and so on.

The written word is immensely precious. It has been the chief carrier of our civilization. Because it can be easily and cheaply gone back over, kept, studied, moved about, referred to, it has an edge over the spoken word which even in the age of electronic sound-recording it shows no sign of losing. But its particular virtue is also the catch in it: being improvable, it needs to be improved as far as you can take the process, or it will work against you, troubling your readers. Use it observantly, though, and it will present you as you want to be presented.

2
THREE GUIDING PRINCIPLES

The bars, theatres and dance halls closed at a minute before midnight every Saturday night, and not a whisky was sold again, not a hip was wriggled, not a bet was placed, until two in the morning on Monday. The Sunday sounds of Dawson City were psalms and snores. No kind of work was allowed. Men were arrested for fishing on a Sunday, or for sawing wood. The only hope of living it up, between Saturday night and Monday morning, was to take a boat downriver and slip across the line into the States—out of reach of the Pax Britannica and its stern schoolmarm values.

James Morris, *Pax Britannica*, Faber & Faber, 1968; chapter 20

Morris's description of a western Canadian Sunday in the 1890s seems to me to exhibit three virtues in particular.

First, it is pictorial. Again and again it calls up specific sights; specific sounds, too. General terms are sparse. The writer doesn't say 'places of entertainment' and 'forms of entertainment', even though that kind of phrase would make sure nothing was left out. Instead three places and three forms are itemized, and the reader's inward eye is instantly engaged.

The Sunday substitutes, going to church or staying in bed, are made present to the mind's ear in a single weighty syllable each: psalms, snores. The ban on any Sunday work (given emphasis in a sudden short sentence) is at once precisely illustrated by the examples about fishing and sawing. Never mind that the list of proscribed activities can't be complete: the writer has sketched pictures, and the reader is happy to fill them in.

Second, the description is vernacular. You could speak it. 'Two in the morning', 'living it up', 'slip across the line', 'schoolmarm values'—these are not terms which belong in some special, lofty language appropriate only to writing. There is no such language. They are phrases which the author and many other people might well use, depending on their hearers, in ordinary talk.

And third, the description gives the reader no trouble. Although it uses colloquialisms, it contains nothing that a reader could reasonably object to. It breaches none of the conventions observed by other good modern writers. Most important, it can be immediately understood. The reader never need go back and try again.

The three guiding principles to which I shall regularly recur in this book are not rules; but they can be enormously helpful in all kinds of writing—personal, scholastic, functional, journalistic, imaginative. They are that you should think in pictures; write as you speak; and keep your reader happy.

THINK IN PICTURES

Have no nonsense with any lingering notion that the written word is in some way inferior to television because television has the pictures. There are no pictures so sharp and apt as the pictures punched up in the reader's mind by sheer words. But to take advantage of them there are things you need to do.

You need to think of your material as illustrating your theme, and to choose both accordingly: usually the theme before the material, but sometimes the theme in the light of the material. Those choices are made before you write a word—at the stage of planning, which we address in the next two chapters. You will seldom say everything there is to be said about a subject: indeed, you would be a super-being if you did. Instead you will often benefit from treating your material as a series of scenes, successive glimpses of the truth, which one by one bring out your theme.

Once you come to write, you will want to make the detail of those scenes pointed and vivid. We consider that process in the third part of the book. One technique is to introduce, as Morris does here, the example that the reader can apprehend with the senses of the mind. Another is to draw out certain qualities in one thing by comparing it to another. You can do that with a metaphor; as Morris does in likening the British empire to a schoolmarm; or as Bacon does when he begins his essay on revenge (1625) by treating justice as a garden herb, useless if it runs wild. 'Revenge is a kind of wild justice; which the more man's nature runs to, the more ought law to weed it out.'

WRITE AS YOU SPEAK

By this I mean that you should try to write as you would speak if you were talking at the top of your form, unhesitantly, in the idiom that best suited your theme and the occasion, and trusting your own ear. Moreover, you should punctuate on much the same system, marking pauses where you would pause in speech to make your meaning clear.

Most of that is in the first part of the book. At the start of the third part we also look at speech rhythms, especially as a means to emphasis.

KEEP YOUR READER HAPPY

With all that, you would be wise to see that you give no avoidable offence. Once you have got something down on paper, take full advantage of the special quality of the written word—that it can be revised. Go over what you have written to make sure that, while it remains sayable, it falls within the current educated conventions about spelling and grammar. At that point no sensible writer does without dictionaries (unless locked in an exam room and obliged to do without them).

More than all, it is vital to ensure that everything you have written can be understood at first reading. A second revision after a lapse of time is useful here: it helps you apply the fresh mind that will be brought to bear by other people.

These aids to the reader's contentment are dealt with in the second part of the book. Without them, you risk throwing away your reader's willingness to stay with you. And without that, you're wasting your time.

3
BEFORE YOU BEGIN

For the past three weeks I have been reporting the war in East Pakistan for the *Sunday Times* in the company of a BBC television unit; five months ago I reported a 'stop smoking' luxury cruise through the Caribbean in the company of an American film crew. I should like to argue from these two experiences—where camera and I had precisely the same raw material to make into films and articles— that as a general rule television is better than words in newspapers at communicating wars, and words are better than television at communicating peace.

Nicholas Tomalin, 'Tactics of reporting', *The Listener*, 29 April 1971; reprinted in *Nicholas Tomalin Reporting*, André Deutsch, 1975

Beginning like that, with a statement of the case he was about to argue and the reason why he wanted to argue it just then, Nicholas Tomalin went on to argue it: a classic opening, followed up with his customary grace and force.

There is now no way of discovering how that particular thought had developed. In October 1973 Tomalin was killed reporting another war for the *Sunday Times*, the Yom Kippur War in Israel. But it looks from the article as if his service as an observer of wars and journalists had already persuaded him of his thesis, and two recent experiences had supplied him with fresh illustration to support it. So he planned and wrote his piece.

Sometimes the preparatory process happens the other way round: the evidence comes before the thesis. You have to write on a certain subject; you accumulate random items of information about it; you ask yourself what theme they support, what sentence they could be summed up in; and you arrange your material round that.

This making of a plan is the most important stage in almost any piece of writing. It is also the stage most often skimped. Hazlitt (in *Table Talk*, 1821) says: 'I seldom see my way a page or even a sentence beforehand'. There are many like him still. But Hazlitt wrote out of an extraordinarily well equipped mind. Unless you are in his class, you would be wise to fortify yourself with a plan.

You may let yourself off in a private letter. 'We go on copying music for you, when we can pick up anything we like. And tell me WHAT SORT OF FRILLS you want for your jacket; I asked you once before; and we might as well set to to do it, if you have not time. Well! to return to Sunday—only *don't forget to answer me these questions*. Mr Steinthal preached on Sunday morning . . .' Thus Mrs Gaskell, the Manchester novelist, writing in 1851 to her 17-year-old daughter Polly; and Polly will have relished the unpremeditatedness, as transcribing her mother's own voice. Your personal letters are a pleasure to read precisely to the extent that they disclose you as you are; absence of forethought may help to that end, unless you have something complicated to say. (Your friends and relations will in any case prefer disorganized letters to none at all.)

In much of your writing, though, you will be addressing a teacher, a senior colleague, an editor, a group of readers you have no personal acquaintance with. These people will as a rule be less interested in you than in your material. Your concern is to present that to the best effect. To that end you must first marshal it properly.

A simple enough procedure is to take a piece of paper, head it something noncommittal like 'points', and list—in any order—the things you want to get in. From this list you remind yourself of, or modify, or identify, your theme—the main point you want to get across, expressible in a sentence or a short paragraph.

Then you take a second piece of paper, head it 'summary', and reorder the points in such a way as to support the theme.

You can of course do that kind of reordering even more easily with a word-processor than with pen and paper: word-processors are clever at the tidy rearranging of sequences, whether they are sequences of words, sentences or paragraphs. Don't feel deprived, though, if you haven't got a word-processor. It might not in the end be an aid to coherence. Being able to waft sentences and paragraphs about like a magician may tempt you into supposing that you can just as well put your thoughts into order after writing them as before. You can't. Sentences or paragraphs written before you have settled your theme cannot support it as neatly as they might; sentences or paragraphs written to fit logically into one context will not fit into another, unless you rewrite them. Patchwork prose-writing, whether you do it with a word-processor or with scissors and paste, can land you either in muddle or—if you are to avoid that—in double labour.

Similarly, it is at this planning stage that you achieve whatever degree of brevity will be a prudent attention to your reader. Having decided the essential points of your theme, you determine the minimum tally of instances and persuasions needed to support each of them, given the kind of space you have been allotted or think appropriate. Once you have written, you will still be able to trim a phrase here and there; but a decent brevity will already have been won without loss of coherence. If

13

on the other hand your method is to write down anything that might be germane and then cut the piece to length—or, worse still, give opportunity to someone else to cut it—by leaving chunks out, such logical sequence as there was will disappear, and you will find that you have covered certain points at disproportionate length and certain points not at all.

There is no substitute for a detailed plan. Even Hazlitt, setting off without one, acknowledged that he was sometimes guilty of 'ill-pieced transitions', and was sometimes obliged to write his essays twice.

Methodical preliminary note-making has another merit: it can ease you through that near-universal affliction, writer's block. You don't have to sit frozen in front of a blank sheet of paper, afraid to sully it with the wrong word. You defer choices about phrasing: you play grandmother's footsteps with them, pretending (if you like) that you're not at present interested. On your first piece of paper you have written down anything that's germane, in any order and words. On your second you tidy the order, but not the words. When I'm in especially cowardly mood I call this summary a draft summary, and do another summary after that; and at that stage the words too are coming tidier, and you're sliding into composition before you know it.

4
TWO MAIN SHAPES

In his Derbyshire home on No. 3 Level, Deadwater Leadmine (disused), near Bakewell, Julian Birdbath, last citizen of the Republic of Letters, sits at his rusting typewriter, with only his pet toad Amiel for company.

But now the never-ceasing, ringing plop of water falling down the stalactite-hung walls seems to sound, in place of its customary knell of despair, a tune of hope.

Yesterday a neighbour, a poultry-farmer and part-time literary agent, shouted down the shaft the news that the Government's Public Lending Right Bill, by which authors will get a fee on any of their books which may be borrowed, had received a second reading in the Lords.

Peter Simple's Way of the World 1975–1977; reprinted from the *Daily Telegraph*

If you have to write something about the public lending right—a thing that few besides authors find interesting—you may shrink from starting cold with a statement of your chosen theme: that it is a lifeline to people who will otherwise drown, perhaps, or that it is an unwarranted second subsidy to people who for the most part are already bankrolled by universities or newspapers.

15

You may therefore prefer, as Peter Simple does in his cod news item, to go straight to an illustration. Think first in pictures: solicit your reader's interest in a particular case, and only then propound the general truth which justifies the solicitation. It works. Julian Birdbath and Amiel are such an intriguing vision that they make you want to keep reading even after you have discovered that the piece is really about the public lending right.

When you are arranging your material before you write, the main question you have to settle is where—having chosen it— you should place your theme. There: that general proposition is my theme for this chapter. I had two broad choices: either to crack straight off with it, or to start with an illustration—the public lending right. I chose the second method; so my theme came in my third paragraph (this one).

In the United States, where the formal teaching of writing (especially journalistic writing) is more developed than it is in Britain, students learn that those two different methods have names: the inverted pyramid, or the *Wall Street Journal* formula.

In an inverted pyramid, you start with the most important thing you have to say: your theme. That's the broad top, at the top of your paper. It may be a generalization, a conclusion from evidence you're about to present. If you're giving directions, it may be an explanation and a summary combined. 'BRUSSELS SPROUT SOUP. The flavour of Brussels sprouts in soup can be too cabbage-like and strong, unless it is softened with potato, celeriac, or potato and a stalk of celery' (*Jane Grigson's Vegetable Book*, 1978).

You then bring in the rest of your material, in tapering order of importance: in a recipe the ingredients, then how to put them together, then how to heat the result, then how to serve it. The method is much used by newspaper reporters: 'The Lords yesterday gave a second reading . . .', then the main things said in the Lords, then the likely next stages, then the story so far, then subsidiary things said. It has the crude practical virtue that sub-editors can cut from the bottom, or readers come away before the end, without great harm being done.

A perfectly sensible variant is to place your pyramid right way up instead. Start at the top with the small stuff and broaden down to the big stuff, the things you really want to say. It is a technique often used by civil servants. They begin with their arguments, sometimes in increasing order of weight; and at the end they crush the reader with their conclusions.

The snag is that before then the reader may have slipped away, bored. The upside-down pyramid is the safer bet: your readers have at least taken in the main point before you lose them. But that risk of losing them remains. Pyramids either way up are not spellbinders. That's why many journalists, knowing how fragile a reader's concentration is, turn for preference to the *Wall Street Journal* formula. Peter Simple uses it in our text. He would scorn the name, I dare say; and the *Wall Street Journal* would not claim to have invented the technique—only to have used it a good deal on the paper's front page, to make feature stories about the soya bean harvest readable.

Under this formula, you begin with the particular instance, the graphic example, often personal: Julian Birdbath, or a named soya bean farmer in Kansas. You sketch his circumstances. Then, just as the reader is beginning to say 'This is interesting, but why am I reading it?', you introduce the paragraph which answers that question by presenting your theme.

American journalists have a name for that paragraph too: the nut graph. (A variant phrase is the fat graph.) Get the nut graph in the right place, and your problem of arrangement is on its way to being solved.

There are of course other possible shapes. Your theme may be a sentence which is never written out, but merely followed as a thread. It might be, for example, the thought that although some people like their pease porridge hot (first group of paragraphs), and others prefer it cold (second group), connoisseurs think it best in the pot, nine days old (final group).

But one thing is common to all those shapes. Whether by giving an illustration, stating your conclusion, putting forward your first argument, or simply offering the first in a sequence of related points, you are starting at once with the matter in hand. That's important. Don't step back: wade in. If you're writing about varying ways of eating pease porridge, don't start by saying that eating habits in general vary. Still less say that human beings vary, and as a sign of that their eating habits vary, and as a sign of that . . . You're not writing about eating in general, nor about human nature, and if you seem to be you're misleading your readers. Get stuck straight into the porridge.

5
HEAR IT IN THE HEAD

I am in good health and have ample private means. I have few bad habits, apart from my sharp tongue. I have no religion, but I observe certain rules of conduct with considerable piety. I feel quite deeply, I think. If I am not very careful, I shall grow into the most awful old battle-axe.

That is why I write, and why I have to. When I feel swamped in my solitude and hidden by it, rendered invisible, in fact, writing is my way of piping up. Of reminding people that I am here.

Anita Brookner, *Look at Me*, Jonathan Cape, 1983; chapter 1

Even so careful a stylist as Anita Brookner derives benefit in this novel from allowing her narrator, a solitary writer, to write as she might speak. Once you have assembled your material, and arranged it in order, and settled down to compose actual sentences, the most useful maxim to keep in mind is this: listen to your words in your head, to make sure that in the appropriate context you could speak them.

That 'I think', in the Brookner passage, is an afterthought— not as a rule a sign of ordered prose; yet it conveys a touch of wry and damaging honesty. A sentence without a verb in ('Of reminding people that I am here') is a device of common speech,

19

untroublesome as long as the meaning is clear, for drawing attention to a few words which might otherwise be no more than a clause in a longer sentence. 'The most awful old battle-axe', 'piping up', 'why I have to': these phrases show in greater detail how within a generally formal style ('I observe certain rules of conduct with considerable piety') the occasional colloquialism enjoys a special emphasis. And this emphasis is added to the emphasis that all three of those phrases take from standing at the end of a sentence, where the main stress of speech ordinarily falls.

Anita Brookner uses the same double-emphasis device to notable effect a few pages later: before she itemizes the 'extremely peculiar décor' of her inherited flat—'terrible cut-glass mirrors with bevelled edges hanging from chains over tiled fireplaces, shaggy off-white fitted carpets, zig-zag patterned rugs, nests of walnut tables...'—she says it 'looks like something sprung direct from the brain of an ambitious provincial tart'. The word 'tart' is given an extra kick not just by its place in the sentence but by the fact of following two words of a careful dignity.

There is a well known passage of Eliot, towards the end of 'Little Gidding' (from *Four Quartets*, 1943), where he says that if your common and your formal words are to form a 'consort dancing together', the common word must be 'exact without vulgarity'. I'm not sure. Vulgarity can spring a pleasurable surprise.

That is not to say that you should lard your writing with colloquialisms, except in rare contexts, like a private letter to someone who shares your mode of speech. Eliot is right about exactitude, and much slang is inexact: playground buzz-words, for example, applicable to anything that rates praise or dispraise. The schoolboy narrator of Salinger's *The Catcher in the Rye* (1951), with his 'terrific' and 'lousy', is equipped for self-revelation, but not precision. 'She looked up at me and sort of smiled. She had a terrifically nice smile. She really did. Most people have hardly any smile at all, or a lousy one.'

And you don't need to go in for constant elisions—like 'don't'. It seems to me that they suit this book, a fairly informal dialogue with a like-minded reader. But if you move up into a more formal register where you think they're out of place, write the sentence another way. Instead of 'where you think they're out of place', write 'where you *find them* out of place'.

The result can still be speakable. Shaw sometimes used elisions: youre, thats, wont (defiantly unapostrophe'd). More often his faultless inner ear allowed him to leave words unelided. Listen to the exchange near the end of *Man and Superman* (1903), after Jack Tanner's reluctant betrothal:

RAMSDEN. You are a happy man, Jack Tanner. I envy you.
MENDOZA. Sir: there are two tragedies in life. One is to lose your heart's desire. The other is to gain it. Mine and yours, sir.
TANNER. Mr Mendoza: I have no heart's desires. Ramsden: it is very easy to call me a happy man: you are only a spectator. I am one of the principals; and I know better. Ann: stop tempting Tavy, and come back to me.
ANN (*complying*). You are absurd, Jack. (*She takes his offered arm.*)
TANNER (*continuing*). I solemnly say that I am not a happy man. Ann looks happy; but she is only triumphant, successful, victorious. That is not happiness, but the price for which the strong sell their happiness.

Eleven possible occasions for elision are there passed by in hardly more than the same number of lines. Yet natural speech is perfectly preserved.

Notice, too, in that passage (which I quote by leave of the

21

Society of Authors on behalf of the Bernard Shaw Estate) how the different marks of punctuation, ranging in weight from comma up through semicolon to full stop, mark the varying lengths of time for which the speaker would most naturally pause in speech. (That point comes up in more detail in chapter 8.) You can also see how the rhythms of speech show, even on the page, where Shaw wanted emphasis to fall. (That technique is explained in chapter 22 and chapter 23.)

Speech is your most serviceable guide. You need not fear that it will betray you into using unsuitable words or phrases or constructions. The fact is that we all speak in several different registers or styles. We use different forms according to whether we're treating frivolous matters, or technical, or solemn; and whether we're talking to a single friend, or a group of colleagues, or a roomful of strangers. The same with writing. As you write, therefore, and as you revise, ask yourself the question: could I say that, aloud, to this audience?

6
THE VIRTUES OF SPEECH

Our section was supposed to be responsible for securing the headquarters from the incursions of enemy agents who might pry out its secrets or subvert its personnel. This gave us a free hand to go almost anywhere and do almost anything. If we went drinking in pubs, it was to keep a look-out for suspicious characters: if we picked up girls, it was to probe their intentions in frequenting the locality. A fellow-officer told me of how, on a pub-crawl, ostensibly a security reconnaissance, he got drunk, and, as was his way when in such a condition, pretended to be a foreigner, using strange gestures and speaking with a broken accent. The next day, badly hung over, he was sent a report of the movements of a suspicious foreigner, and told to check up on them. Tracing the suspect's movements from pub to pub, it slowly dawned on him he was following himself the night before.

Malcolm Muggeridge, *Chronicles of Wasted Time*, volume 2, Collins, 1973; chapter 2

Muggeridge's recollection of wartime intelligence duties shows how you can write as you speak and still use a different tone according to the context. Within the same sentence he can modulate from his own unaffected colloquialisms ('went drinking in pubs', 'picked up girls', 'hung over') to the jargon of the milieu he found himself in ('suspicious characters', 'their intentions in frequenting the locality', 'check up on').

(A minor blemish on the passage is the dangling participle at the beginning of the last sentence. The reader expects 'Tracing' to go with the subject of the main verb; yet the subject, when it comes, turns out to be not 'he' but 'it'. The point recurs in chapter 19.)

So far I have sought to show that conversational writing is something that good writers do in fact engage in. Let me now try to explain what advantages they get from it.

As long as you are sensitive to context (and don't jolt the reader by slighting the logic of sentence-construction), writing as you speak will give you several benefits. First, because the talker is more conscious than the writer of the need to be interesting as well as clear, a conversational style will help you reach for illustration. Muggeridge himself declares in the earlier volume of his autobiography that he is 'temperamentally incapable of understanding anything abstractly stated'. His prose shows him thinking in pictures all the time. The drinking in pubs, the picking up girls, are the graphic instances that will clinch, in the reader's mind, the idea of total licence that Muggeridge is putting across. To say merely 'This gave us total licence', and leave it at that, would be far less effective.

Second, writing as you speak will help you get words out on to the paper. Just as making successively more detailed synopses can ease you almost unaware into your first sentence, so the question 'What would I say if I were simply talking—now?' can pull you through difficult passages.

Third, and perhaps most important, prose that sounds like speech will remind your readers that what they are reading was written by a human being; and this will make them read it more sympathetically. Certain kinds of writing—bureaucratic, social-scientific, even journalistic—often seem to have been written by a robot, reaching for prepared phrases, recoiling from idiosyncrasy. Yet the sense of a human heart beating through plain words can penetrate a reader's indifference as nothing else can.

You get that sense in Bunyan's account (in the first part of *The Pilgrim's Progress*, 1678) of Christian and Hopeful caught trespassing by Giant Despair: 'So they were forced to go, because he was stronger than they. They also had but little to say, for they knew themselves in a fault. The giant therefore drove them before him, and put them into his castle, into a very dark dungeon, nasty and stinking to the spirits of these two men. Here then they lay from Wednesday morning till Saturday night without one bit of bread, or drop of drink or light, or any to ask how they did.'

Fourth, the language of speech authenticates what you write. Tom Wolfe, the American reporter, in his articles about combat flying (a couple of them reprinted in his 1982 collection *The Purple Decades*), makes constant use of aviators' private vocabulary, old and new: 'cob it' for accelerate, 'whifferdill around' for fly aimlessly, 'punch out' for eject, 'get yours' or 'buy it' or 'auger in' or 'crunch' for die.

The context, or a subsidiary phrase, interprets; and the cumulative effect is to persuade the reader that Wolfe has listened to these young men at some length, and hence has a sound base for the important part of his evidence, which is about the state of mind in which they face 'the *daily routine* of risking one's hide'.

And fifth, writing derived from speech keeps the language alive and comprehensive by topping it up with new words. How new words, or new uses of old words, pass into the common vocabulary is a mystery; but speech is ordinarily part of the process. In politics, a pursuit dependent on talk, a new term often appears first in speech: the noun 'wet', lifted from unspecific boarding-school slang and given specific meaning as applied to a non-monetarist Conservative in the Thatcher era,

25

was first given currency in the gossip of the Palace of Westminster. In the world of computers, a coinage like 'byte'—meaning, I learn, a group of eight binary digits—may well have existed first in writing: indeed, if the Barnhart *Dictionary of New English* is right that it's a kind of acronym for *binary digit eight*, it could not have been understood at first except in writing; but it will then have passed from technical papers into the speech of the technicians who read them.

Circulating only in the world of politics or computers, both 'wet' and 'byte' still belonged in private vocabularies. The people who brought them out into the common vocabulary, learning them mostly from speech, were not lexicographers but ordinary writers, attentive to the changing usage of the world they chronicled, and recording it in magazines or advertisements or thrillers. Dictionaries take the new words on from there. Taking care always to be understood, the humblest writer can have a part in that process.

7
ACTIVE WRITING

To take the cuttings, which is best done in September or October, you choose young shoots which have ripened during the summer, and either pull them away from the parent stem with a heel, or cut them off close below one of their own nodes or joints. Anything up to 15 inches is a good length. Take off the lower leaves and the soft unripened tips, set your cuttings upright in a sandy trench which you will previously have prepared with a spade, press them very firmly into the sand, fill in the trench, stamp the soil down, and leave it until the cuttings have formed their roots, when they can safely be transplanted.

V. Sackville-West's *Garden Book*, Michael Joseph, 1968; chapter 3

Everybody has to write directions at some time or other; and, like everything else, you can do it well or badly. Vita Sackville-West shows that the way to do it with the necessary precision is to use plain, one-syllable words as far as possible, but not to shrink from specialist terms as long as they are clear: 'heel' the readers can work out for themselves (especially once they have pulled a shoot away and seen its foot-shaped appendage), 'nodes' needs only a swift alternative as explanation. And in particular she uses active verbs.

In those 114 words, there are 17 verbs. Only two of them are in the passive voice ('is . . . done', 'be transplanted'). The other 15 are all in the active voice. Of those, one is 'is' and one is 'can', which hardly count. The remaining 13 are all genuine verbs of doing ('pull', 'cut', 'press'). Further, only one of those is intransitive, not taking an object ('have ripened'). All the others have an object.

Transitive verbs are a prime tool in effective writing, and English is especially rich in them. Shakespeare uses them constantly. 'The law allows it, and the court awards it', says Portia, in the trial scene in *The Merchant of Venice* (*c.* 1596). Subject, transitive verb, object, twice round.

There is a pre-condition, though. Portia knows her stuff. She has been well briefed (by the lawyer she is replacing, one Bellario). Speaking or writing in active verbs calls for the confidence that comes from knowledge. The passive voice is often the refuge of uncertainty. If I say that creditors *are allowed* to use force in collecting debts, I do not need to say who or what allows it: the law, local custom, the police, the absence of police; and that enables me to disguise the fact that I don't know, or am not sure, or don't want to say. Which may be convenient, but doesn't make for good, clear writing.

That you should know your stuff before you write is of course a counsel of perfection. No one ever knows enough; indeed, learned men have often discovered that the more you know, the more you know your own ignorance, and the pen freezes in your hand. Often, though, you can't defer writing. Journalists, in particular, have regularly to summon their resolve and feed the machine they work for, whether the state of their knowledge justifies the expense of paper or not. But you can still avoid flabbiness if you think hard about the words in which you put forward such material as you do have. Here are a few instances of what I mean.

Mistrust abstract nouns of no clear meaning. The word 'situation' has already been comprehensively ridiculed; keep the same cold eye on 'aspect', 'element', 'factor', 'feature'. Instead of 'The important aspect (or element, or factor, or feature) of this plan is . . .', at least write 'The important thing about this plan is . . .' You win a point for being plain and unpompous. Better still, write 'What matters about this plan is . . .', or 'This plan matters because . . .' Then you're using an active verb, and you're speaking directly to your reader.

Be careful of comparatives. 'We try harder.' Harder than what? Than our competitors? Than we used to? Than you might expect? That uncertainty is a convenient refuge, sometimes a necessary refuge, for writers of advertisements. But if you're trying to write with decent frankness, ask yourself 'than what?'; and unless the context removes all doubt, put the answer in.

Be sparing of qualifiers. 'This was the noblest Roman of them all', says Antony, in the last scene of *Julius Caesar* (*c.* 1599). He does not say that Brutus was 'probably' (or 'belike', or 'mayhap') the noblest: Antony is sure of his reasons for the claim, and goes on to list them. If he had not been sure, he would have done better to stay away from the superlative altogether. Nor does he say 'quite simply the noblest': 'noblest' is the top of the range, and extra words can't push it higher than that. 'Quite', in general, is a word to avoid. Confusion can arise between its two senses, 'completely' and 'fairly'. (If a theatre is quite full, is it packed or part-empty?) And in the 'fairly' sense you ought not to need it; nor that other timid qualifier, 'rather'. Instead of picking too strong an adjective and having to weaken it, choose an accurate one and let it stand by itself. Instead of 'rather precipitous', write 'steep'. And don't imagine that you're any better off with 'not unprecipitous'. It is as limp-wristed, as non-active, a turn of phrase as you could find. (Orwell, in a footnote to his 1946 essay on 'Politics and the English language', wrote: 'One can cure oneself of the *not un-* formation by memorizing this sentence: *A not unblack dog was chasing a not unsmall rabbit across a not ungreen field.'*)

And watch punctuation—our next subject. Look back for a moment to Vita Sackville-West, and notice the punctuation of the two relative clauses in the last whole sentence. No commas before 'which you will previously have prepared with a spade', because it identifies the trench, and you would not pause after 'trench' in speaking; but a comma before 'when they can safely be transplanted', because it doesn't identify the moment of root-formation, and in speech you would pause. I shall return to that distinction. By neglecting it, many writers deny their readers necessary guidance.

8
PUNCTUATION AS TIMING

For the few days that were left to the family, Joseph now became their mascot. In the relief of Alastair's departure, they adopted him wholeheartedly. Lucy propositioned him; he declined, courteously, even regretfully. She passed the sad news to Pauly, who met with a somewhat firmer rejection: further impressive proof that he was sworn to chastity. Until Alastair's departure, the family had been contemplating a slackening of their lives together. Their little marriages were breaking up, fresh combinations were not saving them; Lucy thought she might be pregnant, but then Lucy often did, and with reason.

John le Carré, *The Little Drummer Girl*, Hodder & Stoughton, 1983; chapter 3

Punctuation records pauses. Broadly, a comma marks a count of one, a semicolon of two, a colon of three and a full stop of four. Le Carré is a careful writer, in this as in other things. If he were to take this passage (about the group of actors from among whom his heroine is kidnapped for a counter-terrorist task) and read it aloud, his pauses would follow that notation.

That is the basis of accurate and helpful punctuation: listen to your words in your head, and mark the pauses you hear. Then you will keep your reader with you.

You will also find that you are keeping the rules, the reigning conventions. A count of one, the weight of a comma, is a very brief gap in time. So the job of separating sentences—in the sense of groups of words with a main, not a subordinate, verb in—is ordinarily left to the heavier stops: semicolon, colon, full stop. The main verbs in the first half of the le Carré passage are 'became', 'adopted', 'propositioned', 'declined' and 'passed'; and they are all separated by one of those three stops. ('Were left', 'met' and 'was sworn' are all in subordinate clauses.)

The semicolon is an elegant stop, under-used: it indicates a strong logical link between the two sentences it separates. ('Lucy propositioned him; he declined . . .') A colon can do the same job, with a fractionally longer pause, and it has another useful property besides: it can say 'as follows', 'and this is what I mean'—as it has done twice already in this paragraph. It introduces an extension or an explanation, not necessarily with a verb in. That is how le Carré uses it here.

A single dash can do the same job, and it can also add a calculated afterthought. But it has its drawbacks. Both in typewriting and in print the dash is sometimes confused with the hyphen. This confusion ought not to arise. In typewriting, the dash is best represented by a double hyphen, standing free (as the hyphen does not) of the words on either side. In print, the dash is either of that form (about twice a hyphen's length, and free-standing) or of the form used in this book (about four times a hyphen's length, and joined). But typists and compositors don't always observe those distinctions, and the reader is briefly bewildered.

The single dash carries another slight handicap. Many people seem to have been taught in youth that using it is in some way slovenly; and some of them have not outgrown the instruction. A reader once wrote to me to recall a typist who had terrorized him on the point. Another reader, apparently a schoolmaster, considered dashes a reason for docking marks. This animus against dashes has no foundation in good usage: many first-rate writers—Hazlitt, Ruskin, Lytton Strachey—make extensive use of the single dash. Nevertheless, it is a pity to irritate even wrong-headed readers needlessly, especially if they happen to be your examiners. All in all, for our purpose of introducing an elucidation, it is probably prudent to follow this practice: use a colon where you can, and use a dash only where a colon won't do—as in this sentence, where a colon has appeared once already.

(A brace of dashes, as I have used it in the third and sixth paragraphs of this chapter to enclose a certain kind of interpolation, is a different thing altogether. Its turn comes in chapter 10.)

Although commas don't ordinarily separate sentences (in the sense of groups of words with main verbs in), there are two kinds of occasion when they do. The first is when the comma is followed by a conjunction, an 'and', a 'but': 'Lucy thought she might be pregnant, but then Lucy often did . . .' There is no basis in good usage for the belief, oddly widespread, that 'and' and 'but' ought never to have commas before them. Le Carré is only one of countless good writers who often mark a pause before 'and' or 'but'. Frequently sense and rhythm demand it, and the sentence overall—between full stops—would be clumsy without. Sometimes the pause needs to be of the weight of a semicolon or a full stop. (The Authorized Version of the Bible often starts a sentence with 'and' after a full stop, and fairly often after a semicolon.)

The second occasion when sentences may be separated with commas is when the sentences are parallel, and would be spoken with parallel inflections: 'Their little marriages were breaking up, fresh combinations were not saving them . . .' Again and again, punctuation is governed by the sound on the inner ear.

The most common mistake made with commas, often by

professional writers, concerns the punctuation of relative clauses. There are two relative clauses in the le Carré passage: 'that were left to the family', and 'who met with a somewhat firmer rejection'. The first defines 'the few days': it is of the type grammarians sometimes call restrictive or essential. It takes no comma before it, for the sufficient reason that in speech you would not pause before it.

The second does not define Pauly: it simply gives fresh information about him. It is of the type called non-restrictive or non-essential. It needs its comma, because in speech you would pause before it. Yet that comma is again and again left out; and the reason why the omission is a mistake is that it befogs the reader. 'He kissed the girl who slapped him': sense, and sound, quite different from the same sentence with a comma in. (Without the comma, the slap precedes the kiss: with the comma, the kiss comes first.) Listen to what you write, and you will be delivered from error.

9
THE GENITIVE SOUND

Its promoter was a stout aristocrat, Henry Jermyn, Earl of St Albans, who, having supported Charles I's widow, Henrietta Maria, through miserable years of exile in France (and, according to some, actually married her), returned in 1660 and forthwith acquired rights over St James's; the success of his speculation was secured by the gravitation westward of moneyed householders after the Great Fire of 1666, and St James's became the fashionable address for many of Charles II's courtiers, including his mistresses. Though it has its half-concealed crevices and inconsequential yards, the plan of St James's is still much as laid out, and it *is* a plan, about the symmetry of the Square itself. Only Inigo Jones's venture in Covent Garden precedes it in date.

David Piper, *The Companion Guide to London*, Collins, 6th edition, 1977; chapter 4, 'St James's'

Wisely, David Piper writes the name of that neighbourhood of London in exactly the way most people pronounce it: St James's—Jame-ziz. Yet many people find writing that kind of name difficult. I live in a small street in another part of London called St James's Walk. That's how it appears in Post Office lists, and how we give it out. But it defeats most of our correspondents. We get James, James', Jame's, Jamess; on a rate demand from the town hall we have had Jamés, with an acute accent.

The hospital across the river from the Houses of Parliament has its name cut into concrete outside, and printed on its letterhead, as St Thomas'. Yet on the letterhead of the hospital's medical school the name appears as St Thomas's.

It seems to me that the medical school has the better of it; and for no other reason than that the school spelling represents what people actually say. Evidently, there is a doubt about how to write the possessive or genitive form of names ending in s or x or z. The best argument to settle the doubt is the argument from current speech: your own speech. If you put the apostrophe-s on in speech, put it on in writing. If not, not.

Part of the beauty of this advice is that there need be no exceptions to it. David Piper writes 'Inigo Jones's' because (I don't doubt) he says 'Inigo Jones's'. So would I. If you find it natural to say 'Jesus's parables', 'Dickens's novel', 'Socrates's method', then write it. If not, go another way to work: 'the parables of Jesus', 'a Dickens novel' (where 'Dickens' is used as an adjective), 'the Socratic method'.

The alternative, widely followed, is the St Thomas' Hospital solution: 'Jesus'', 'Dickens'', without the final s. (A reputable school of thought advocates this for all biblical and classical names.) If you adopt this course, though, remember that an aspostrophe is silent. Writing 'Jesus' parables' is the equivalent of saying 'Jesus parables', which may not immediately make sense. Writing 'Dickens' novels' also invites the printer to commit the indefensible though surprisingly common trans-position, 'Dicken's'.

A silent apostrophe and nothing else is fine in a phrase like 'for goodness' sake', because that is how everybody says it. And of course it is almost universally used in genitive plurals: old wives' tale, the Joneses' party, seven days' journey. (The last is a descriptive genitive: a journey of seven days; but it's still a

36

genitive.) The chief exceptions are the genitives of nouns with irregular plurals: women's, people's.

Apostrophes arouse disproportionate passions. I once heard a good writer arguing earnestly that the possessive apostrophe should be applied to people only, and not to things: that you might write 'St James's Square', but not 'the square's appearance'. Even if he had a case in logic, he had none in usage. A genitive s has been added for four hundred years to things. (Othello: 'It is a sword of Spain, the ice brook's temper . . .')

You may have noticed one other detail in our Piper text: that there is no apostrophe in St Albans—even though Alban, the first British Christian martyr, is as historical a saint as most, and the town is built round his abbey. The fact is that these things are subject to chance and change, and you just have to look them up. In the same county as St Albans, near Ware, there is a place called St Margaret's: tiny, but (for the time being) perfectly apostrophe'd.

I owe that information to the *ABC Rail Guide*, which is meticulous in these matters. It also tells me to write King's Cross, but Potters Bar; and Earl's Court, but Barons Court. Another well of these unfathomable truths is the *Oxford Dictionary for Writers and Editors*, which exists to clear away just those doubts that can arise even in a well stocked mind.

Apostrophes disappear constantly. They have long been disappearing from the names of shops, like Harrods—perhaps partly because graphic artists and the designers of illuminated signs find them a nuisance, particularly in cursive script. They are also being dropped from the names of groups. If you look in the London telephone directory (another scrupulous work) under 'national', you will find several bodies with names like the National Egg Packers Association and even the National Readers Association. You might reasonably expect an apostrophe on the end of 'Packers' (to say nothing for the moment about a hyphen in front) and of 'Readers', since those are associations of packers and readers. But the packers and the readers would probably not thank you for adding the apostrophe. The journalistic maxim that people and organizations should be called what they want to be called is in general the only practicable one.

This patchy disappearance of apostrophes may also follow from the prevailing uncertainty about them. The National Farmers Union, I feel sure, has better reasons for leaving out its apostrophe than a niggling doubt about whether the apostrophe should come before or after the s; but one or two organizations may be shy of committing themselves. You can see a comparable uncertainty in a common misuse of the apostrophe: the greengrocer's plural. This takes an apostrophe where none is needed: 'LETTUCE'S 50p', and so on. ('Even in Jermyn Street I have seen SOCK'S and TIE'S', a reader laments. 'And you can get TEA'S all over the countryside.')

There are a few contexts where plurals are made in that way: witness the playground riddle that ends 'How many s's in that?' And it is possible to argue that an apostrophe in the plural has as much validity as an apostrophe in the genitive, since historically both the plural s and the genitive s represent contractions of longer forms. Nevertheless, in modern English there is a well established convention that, with a few exceptions, plurals don't take an apostrophe and genitives do. (The notable exception among genitives is the first word in the Piper passage, 'its', meaning 'of it', which is distinguished precisely by its lack of apostrophe from the other 'it's', meaning 'it is' or 'it has'.) That convention is helpful to the reader, and therefore deserves to be respected by the writer.

10
PUNCTUATING IN PAIRS

This superiority to death mattered to Donne because death struck him, above all else, as a personal affront. The business of being buried, and decomposing, was, as he observed in his last sermon (when he had finally come to terms with the fact that he was going to rot like everyone else), 'the most inglorious and contemptible vilification'. The question most of us want to ask about death—Is it going to hurt?—never seems to have bothered him. It would have been beneath his dignity to worry about pain. Death was an insult to his ego. It threatened to turn him into an inanimate object. He refused to succumb to it passively, in art as in life.

John Carey, *John Donne: Life, Mind and Art*, Faber & Faber, 1981; chapter 7

You're writing something fairly complicated. You want to follow a clear line of exposition or argument, but you have a lot of detail to take account of along the way. You may well decide to pull some of this detail into your sentences parenthetically, in interpolations: groups of words dropped into a sentence without affecting its main current. Professor Carey, like many literary critics, uses the device a good deal.

An interpolation is separated from the rest of the sentence by punctuation: brackets, dashes or commas; and the essential thing is that the mark of punctuation should be the same at each end. Then the reader can at once see which words, with their outer covering of punctuation, are to be thought of separately. In speech you would make the same point with a pair of pauses; and the double punctuation corresponds.

Yet people often allow the second mark of punctuation to differ from the first, or to disappear altogether. And the reader has to read the sentence twice.

There isn't much problem about brackets (or parentheses, to use the printing term for these curved ones: strictly, brackets are the square or angular ones, though in ordinary usage the same word covers all kinds). Their very shape shows them to be incomplete without both ends. The only doubt people seem to have about brackets is where to put the full stop if an end-bracket coincides with the end of a sentence. The doubt can be simply and logically resolved. If the words in brackets are part of a larger sentence, as they are in the first sentence of this paragraph, then you put the full stop outside, since the full stop concludes the whole sentence, and not just the part of it that's in brackets. But if the words in brackets are themselves a whole sentence or group of sentences, as they are in the last sentence of this paragraph, then you put the full stop inside, because the sentence it concludes is inside. (If the mark of punctuation beside the end-bracket is something less than a full stop, as in Carey's second sentence, then it almost invariably goes outside, as belonging to the sentence as a whole.)

Dashes differ slightly from brackets. The interesting difference is on the ear. If you were to read the Carey passage aloud, you would probably drop your voice at the words between brackets; whereas for the words between dashes you would keep much the same pitch going. That would be a recognition that the question 'Is it going to hurt?' is of equal importance with the other words in the sentence; but that the words about

Donne's state of mind during his last sermon, although valuable as explanation, are not.

But dashes also differ from brackets in that a dash can stand by itself—like this. A single dash is therefore not an evident oddity like a single bracket. That does introduce the risk that, of a pair of dashes, the second will be changed or dropped, and the reader left uncertain where the interpolation ends. Where the system most often goes wrong, though, is with pairs of commas.

In Carey's first sentence there's a comma'd interpolation: 'above all else'. It could almost equally well have no commas: the alternative to a pause at each end is no pauses at all. What would have been confusing is to have a comma at the beginning and not at the end. Yet that happens a lot. The second comma in a pair has become an endangered species.

Carey's second sentence contains two interpolations. The first of them, 'and decomposing', would again make adequate sense if it were not comma'd off at all. But Carey needs the extra emphasis conferred by a pause after the phrase, and he therefore needs one before it as well. The second interpolation is 'as he observed in his last sermon'. This in turn has an insertion in it, at its end: the words in brackets. Carey is still careful to give it its second comma, after the bracket.

Trouble seems most often to arise over those little appositional phrases that explain who people are. 'Sinclair, the Liberal leader, hesitated.' Thus A.J.P. Taylor, impeccably, in his *English History 1914–1945* (1965), about a possible prolonging of the Second World War coalition. Yet from other hands the sentence might now appear as 'Sinclair, the Liberal leader hesitated.' That rhythm would do for 'Suspicious, the Liberal leader hesitated.' But where the phrase 'the Liberal leader' is not the subject of the sentence but just an explanatory insertion, both sound and sense demand the second comma. (There are instances where you can do without either comma. They come up in the last paragraph but two of chapter 14.)

41

A separate point. A few pages before the passage I quote, Carey recalls that Donne (in *Biathanatos*, 1647) called Christ's death 'an heroic act'. Confusion now surrounds that usage: 'an' before an audible h. No problem with 'an honourable man', because that h is silent. But many people understandably hesitate over 'an hotel', 'an historic event', 'an hilarious occasion'.

The same advice applies as with possessives like 'St James's'. If you say it, write it. If you are the kind of person who says 'an hotel', write it. If you are not, have no compunction in leaving out the n in writing. Clearly the usage derives from a time when many more h's than now were silent. My prediction would be that, with more and more h's sounded, 'an hotel' and the rest of them will all but disappear.

II REMEMBERING THE READER

11
BEING UNDERSTOOD AT ONCE

Thirty-five miles east of the drop zones of the American parachutists, and five hours after they had touched earth, the North Shore Regiment of the 3rd Canadian Division started the difficult trans-shipment between the ships in which they had crossed the Channel and those from which they would step out on to the beaches of France. They had come as far as the 'lowering point', seven miles out, in a Landing Ship Infantry (LSI), a converted cross-channel steamer which, in peace, had carried tourists to France. Conversion had meant no more than stripping its sides of lifeboats and replacing their davits with a heavier-duty type, from which could be swung a port and starboard row of LCAs. The Landing Craft Assault was the lowliest class of vessel admitted to the books of the Royal Navy. Commanded by a petty-officer coxswain, it provided nothing but rough benches for 35 men—a platoon of infantry—and a diesel engine just powerful enough to push them ashore at 10 knots.

John Keegan, *Six Armies in Normandy*, Jonathan Cape, 1982; chapter 3

It is good to use the language of the world you're writing about. Readers enjoy it, and trust you the more for it. But they need to understand it at first reading.

At least as important as sounding like yourself is keeping your readers with you. Without that, all the charm of all the Muses goes for nothing. It is to the technique of retaining your readers that we now turn. That technique is not a difficult one: it chiefly demands that you should be aware of your readers as people like yourself, often busy, sometimes inattentive, occasionally irritable, not always sharp-witted or well informed. Think of them like that, and you will never knowingly oblige them to read a sentence twice. You will make sure that they understand your technical terms. You will never leave them in confusion about the reference of a pronoun (a 'they', an 'it'), or about which pairs of words you want taken together as compound adjectives (like 'heavier-duty', in our Keegan text, where dropping the hyphen could easily have caused a stumble). You will never trouble your readers by leaving out those extra words that put the sense beyond doubt, or by avoidably using a construction which you know may be an occasion of offence, or by deploying one of those double-edged words whose old sense is being supplanted by a new one and yet still has its defenders. All those points come up in these next ten chapters.

In his book on the 1944 Normandy landings, John Keegan is scrupulous about explaining his terms. Often he defines them in advance. He does that with 'lowering point': it is the place of the trans-shipment he has just described. He does the same thing with 'platoon'. The benefit is that non-specialist readers then understand the term as soon as they come to it, with no break in their comprehension; and specialists, recognizing the thing from the advance description, are gratified to have their knowledge of the name confirmed, instead of being irritated at finding the name followed by an explanation they don't need.

'Lowering point' is in fact a notably prosaic term for a place of such potential danger. That, I take it, is why Keegan puts quotation-marks round it: to show that this was indeed the term used. He is too good a writer to flag a phrase with quotation-marks as a way of apologizing for it. If a term is comprehensible,

46

it is admissible; and if you nevertheless find that there is something wrong with it, the proper course is to change it, not to try and distance yourself from it with inverted commas. (The inverted-commas trick is particularly favoured by philosophers, as if to suggest that the English language is after all a poor thing to catch the subtlety of their thought. Don't be impressed. Perhaps they haven't searched for the right phrase hard enough.)

When Keegan does interpret a term afterwards, instead of beforehand, as he does with 'converted', he disguises the interpretation as wry comment: conversion was a less thorough business than the name implied. Groups of initials, one of the commonest forms of technical term, he explains both in advance and in arrears: LSI in advance (the more usual method); LCA in arrears, but again concealing the explanation. Either way, he can then go on using the initials plain (and has to, since the word-order of the full name is not the word-order of ordinary speech).

So being understood at once is not necessarily a matter of using short, plain words, vigorous and natural though that can be. Sometimes you can't avoid using long or difficult ones. When that happens, though, both prudence and the example of good writers counsel that you shouldn't make your readers cast around for a work of reference in which to look up the difficult terms.

Certainly it is one of the virtues of the written word, as distinct from the spoken or the broadcast, that those taking it in can stop and think or consult elsewhere and not be left behind. Certainly there are kinds of writing which may decently be difficult. Poetry—loaded with associations by the writer, regularly revisited by the reader—cannot reasonably be expected to deliver up all its secrets first time round. Matter written by the learned for the learned will seldom be pellucid to the unlearned. But difficult or specialized subjects are not in

47

themselves an excuse for difficult prose. Indeed, they make it all the wiser to write as explanatorily as you can.

Of course you have to presume a measure of knowledge. Keegan assumes that his readers know what davits are. That seems fair enough; and anyway the context makes it clear that davits are in some way linked to lifeboats. In general the best practice is to assume, among those interested enough to be your readers, only such knowledge as the least well equipped of them might bring to bear. Beyond that, make sure you supply the gaps; and do it tactfully.

12
SAY IT AGAIN

In fact El Salvador had always been a frontier, even before the Spaniards arrived. The great Mesoamerican cultures penetrated this far south only shallowly. The great South American cultures thrust this far north only sporadically. There is a sense in which the place remains marked by the meanness and discontinuity of all frontier history, by a certain frontier proximity to the cultural zero. Some aspects of the local culture were imposed. Others were borrowed. An instructive moment: at an exhibition of native crafts in Nahuizalco, near Sonsonate, it was explained to me that a traditional native craft was the making of wicker furniture, but that little of this furniture was now seen because it was hard to obtain wicker in the traditional way. I asked what the traditional way of obtaining wicker had been. The traditional way of obtaining wicker, it turned out, had been to import it from Guatemala.

Joan Didion, *Salvador*, Chatto & Windus, 1983; chapter 5

There is virtue in repetition. It can help make your sentences understood at first reading; and it can sometimes do more for them than that. In the paragraph I quote, Joan Didion's phrase about obtaining wicker in the traditional way comes three times in three sentences. The ordinary recourse, the second and third

49

time, would have been to use pronouns. The last two sentences could have read: 'I asked what that had been. It had been, it turned out, to import it from Guatemala.' But then 'it' in the last sentence would have borne three different meanings. Or the two sentences might simply have run: 'What had that been? To import it from Guatemala.' Even then, readers would have had to understand 'that' as referring to the traditional way of obtaining wicker, and 'it' as referring to the wicker itself; which they might not have managed at first reading.

So instead Joan Didion repeats herself. As a result, she achieves a hint of the patient questioning needed, and in the end a pleasing irony. And more than all that, she is clear.

Bulwer-Lytton, the prolific and now largely unread novelist, in a letter he wrote in 1848 to congratulate Macaulay on *The History of England*, held it a peculiarity in Macaulay's style that he repeated nouns. Macaulay replied that he did it on principle; and Macaulay is himself so admirable a technician, and yet one who wrote so seldom about his technique, that his explanation is worth giving at some length. (I find it in the 1982 selection from the great Pinney edition of Macaulay's letters for the Cambridge University Press.)

I repeat nouns that I may not misuse pronouns. There is no fault so common even in our best writers as that of putting *he* and *it* in wrong places. I have taken down Johnson's Lives of the Poets, and I transcribe absolutely at random the very first paragraph on which I open.

'From this time Pope lived in the closest intimacy with his (Pope's) commentator, and amply rewarded his (Warburton's) kindness and zeal; for he (Pope) introduced him (Warburton) to Mr Murray, by whose interest he (Warburton) became preacher at Lincoln's Inn, and to Mr Allen who gave him (Warburton) his (Allen's) niece, and his (Allen's) estate, and by consequence a bishopric. When he (Pope) died, he (Pope) left him (Warburton) the property of his (Pope's) works.'

The whole book, and nine tenths even of the good books in our language, are written in this way. Only look at the last sentence. There is no reason whatever for connecting the *hes* and *hims* with Pope and Warburton rather than with Allen, except that the context guides the reader to the sense. I have a horror almost morbid of this fault. I could compose twice as fast as I do if it were not for the extreme scrupulosity with which I arrange my pronouns.

Not absolutely at random, I come on this corroborative passage from the third chapter of Macaulay's history, about how a late-17th-century cleric might be promoted by his patron from a domestic chaplaincy to a parish, a cure of souls. 'With his cure he was expected to take a wife. The wife had ordinarily been in the patron's service; and it was well if she was not suspected of standing too high in the patron's favour.' Repeating 'wife' and 'patron' makes for clarity; and because of the circumstance (explored in chapter 23) that repeating one word or phrase can lay stress on another near it, the repetition of 'patron' gives sardonic emphasis to the key word 'favour'.

Joan Didion turns the same circumstance to account in the early part of our text. Since the third sentence ('The great South American cultures. . .') picks up a number of words from the second, extra emphasis falls on the words not picked up: especially 'South', 'north' and 'sporadically'.

You may not want that kind of emphasis. If not, repeating a word can weaken that word without countervailing gain elsewhere. Repetition can suggest disorganization (the word 'but' coming twice in quick succession), or inattention (two outings for the same word close together yet in different senses—'Joan Didion has written about six books about her findings as a reporter'), or uninventiveness (the same general term of praise reiterated).

So you will sometimes prefer pronouns (or the adjectives from them—'their', 'its'). When you do, remember Macaulay's morbid horror and make sure your connections are clear. One useful trick to that end is to juggle with gender or number. 'The government told the bank to settle its debts.' Whose debts? As that sentence stands, they could be either side's. But change 'The government' to 'The minister' and the debts are clearly the bank's; or change 'the bank' to 'the directors' and the debts are clearly the government's.

A less acceptable recourse is to use, instead of a pronoun, an alternative description of the person or thing the pronoun stands for. In the passage (it dates from 1781) that Macaulay objects to, Johnson could have substituted 'the satirist' for the first 'he' as applied to Pope, and 'the translator of Homer' for the second. The practice used to be called elegant variation. But Johnson would have known better than to think it elegant, and its 19th-century vogue is over.

I'm afraid the device creeps back, though, in certain kinds of journalistic writing. 'Ramsbottom pounced on the ball. The 19-year-old part-time trombonist steadied himself . . .' The laudable aim there is not to impress the reader with breadth of knowledge but to shoehorn extra information in with as few extra words as possible. The snag is that, because the information does not fit at that point, we suddenly seem to be fronted with a new character. Who is this trombonist? Write like that, and you occasion the very thing you want to avoid: a break in the reader's understanding.

13
THE LITTLE-USED HYPHEN

August Grell re-entered his bedroom, closed the shutters before he turned on the light near his desk, unlocked its top, and rolled it up. Now he reached in to pull out the pigeonholes; they came away in one piece, a screen to block the gap that lay behind. Carefully, he placed this unit against the wall, keeping the pigeonholes upright so that they held their pieces of writing paper and envelopes and bills intact. The desk was old-fashioned and deep; the disclosed gap easily held his communication equipment. It was a strange mixture: the latest in short-wave radio transmitters with tape attached for high-speed receiving and sending (Russian model); a schedule for transmission—kilocycles changed according to the month as well as to the day of the week (an adaptation of the Russian methods that had worked very well in America); the usual one-time cipher pads, with their lists of the false numbers that had been inserted into the code for the sake of security, each small tissue-thin page easily destroyed after it had guided the decoding . . .

Helen MacInnes, *The Salzburg Connection*, Collins, 1969; chapter 2

An indispensable aid to being understood at once is the hyphen. It tells your reader when two words (or parts of words), and sometimes more, go closely together. Especially if those words

53

are meant to form a single, composite adjective before a noun, the reader may trip unless the hyphen is in place. Fowler's *Modern English Usage* (the Gowers edition of 1965) offers as an example, in an excellent entry on hyphens, 'a little-used car'. Leave out the hyphen and the phrase means something quite different. Yet hyphens in composite adjectives are becoming rare: troublesomely rare.

Helen MacInnes uses hyphens a lot. Her usage is worth looking at.

re-entered: untypically, the hyphen as separator rather than joiner. Most words in re-, even (for example) 'reinforce', are commonly written as one; but 'reentered' might puzzle the reader for a moment. Save yourself trivial decisions, and inconsistency, by using a dictionary.

pigeonhole: the Oxford dictionaries prefer 'pigeon-hole', perhaps because if you admit 'pigeonhole' you can hardly refuse 'bolthole' and 'loophole', with the risk that the reader's eye will see the second syllables as '-thole' and '-phole'. Yet there is a natural tendency for two words much in each other's company to end up properly married, as a single word. The question every time is what is least likely to stop the reader; and it is sometimes difficult to answer. I admit that in the MacInnes paragraph before this one I was stopped by 'dripproof', even though it came immediately after the perfectly acceptable 'weatherproof'.

writing paper: the sole lapse here, in my judgment. The reader would have been better served by 'writing-paper'. The same goes for a term like 'sitting-room'. We are dealing here with paper to write on, or a room to sit in; yet the unhyphened form, strictly interpreted, suggests paper that writes and a room that sits. The difference can often be discerned by the ear as well as by reason. Every separate word carries at least one stress. Yet in

54

'sitting-room', the second word is unstressed: it has lost its separateness, and become part of a new compound word. A hyphen helps the reader to perceive that. In 'sitting duck', on the other hand, the second word keeps its stress because it keeps its separateness, and a hyphen would be misleading. Logical hyphenation enables your reader to hear the same groupings of words, the same rhythms, as you hear.

old-fashioned: instead of independently describing the desk, as 'deep' does, the first of these two adjectives qualifies the second. It is the fashion that is old. Then the whole compound is brought to bear, duly hyphened. Yet a few lines before our paragraph begins Helen MacInnes has 'carefully fashioned', with no hyphen. Quite right too: an adverb, like 'carefully', needs no special sign that it is modifying the adjective next to it. That relation can be understood at once. No hyphen is needed, therefore, in 'well known', 'ill advised', and so on.

short-wave, high-speed: adjectives, easily identifiable as such because they come before the things they describe; and composite, therefore to be hyphened. Each is in fact made up of an adjective and a noun. If the noun were being used on its own, and not as part of a compound adjective, no hyphen would be needed. Transmissions on short wave travel at high speed.

one-time, tissue-thin: compound adjectives again, and the important examples. If there were no hyphen, readers might well read 'the usual one' (the usual kind of transmitter), 'each small tissue' (in a pad made up of tissues); and then they would be thrown by the next couple of words, and have to go back. Never send your readers back.

Omission can sometimes lead to an actual change of meaning. This is the 'little-used car' point. In a later passage, Helen MacInnes has 'an English-language magazine' in Tokyo: a magazine in the English language. Drop the hyphen, and the phrase most naturally means an English magazine about language (of which admirable specimens exist). And a girl knits 'a thick-stitched sweater'—a sweater with thick stitches; unhyphened, though, it becomes a thick sweater with stitching on it.

Strictly, that latter meaning would demand 'a thick, stitched sweater', with a comma. But so meticulous a writer as Henry James, in *What Maisie Knew*, has: 'If Maisie had been a mere rough trousered thing'—in other words, if she had been a boy. Presumably James left out the comma because he wanted a rapid rhythm. The modern eye, used to supplying missing hyphens, is tempted to read 'rough-trousered'. But that would alter James's meaning: instead of manner and gender, he would be talking about clothes. Leaving those hyphenable gaps has grown risky.

Another Maisie, in another 1890s novel, Kipling's *The Light that Failed*, appears 'black-velvet-hatted'. Nothing forbids a run of hyphens. Some phrases positively demand it. If 'ex-Labour-MP' becomes 'ex-Labour MP', it no longer means a former Labour MP, it means someone who is still an MP but has switched parties. The phrase 'stained glass-fancier', which I saw recently, would properly describe a messy toper.

A reader has supplied me with a charming example of the way missing hyphens can distort behaviour as well as meaning. She discovered her husband struggling to broach the plastic pot that contained a steak-and-kidney pudding from Marks & Spencer. 'I'm trying to find the clip on the lid', he explained. Together they re-examined the instructions; and sure enough, the first words were: 'Remove clip on lid'. (There were no hyphens in steak-and-kidney, either.)

14
NOT TOO SHORT, PLEASE

And so it is that Petworth comes to the Restaurant Propp, beneath the castle in Slaka, residence once of Bishop-Krakator 'Wencher' Vlam (1678–1738, if my hastily scribbled notes are correct), and meets there the brilliant, batik-clad magical realist novelist Katya Princip, who takes him familiarly by the arm, leads him out of the group, and moves him towards the corner of the room. 'Come now and talk to me,' she says...

[*Then, 94 pages later, as their acquaintance ripens under a shared shower:*] 'Don't you wash me, I think you are very clean.' 'Yes,' says Petworth, 'certainly.' 'You do not know Marx, but I think you know Freud,' says Princip. 'Isn't this water very nice?'

'Yes, I do,' says Petworth, his hands moving over the soft contours of no-longer batik-clad magical realist novelist Katya Princip.

Malcolm Bradbury, *Rates of Exchange*, Secker & Warburg, 1983; chapters 4 and 7

Fifty-two-year-old Leicester-educated master-of-the-running-gag Malcolm Bradbury is here making gentle fun, I take it, of a stylistic device chiefly used by journalists: the cramming in of information, where there is a lot of it to unload, by means of adjectival phrases lined up before a name.

The reason why journalists use it is clear enough: it saves words. Comb all the information out into separate sentences or relative clauses ('Malcolm Bradbury, who's 52, was educated at . . .') and it will take up more room: a little more room, at any rate. When the term 'journalese' was current, it meant verbal inflation, the using of more and longer words than was necessary in an effort after dignity and (if you were paid by the line) money. But the ratio of matter to space has changed. Newspapers regularly have much more to publish than they have room for, unless they compress it. If the word 'journalese' were used now it would most naturally mean a language peculiarly squeezed.

Since this device of multiple adjectives is so widely used by my fellow journalists, and is here given a certain jocular currency by Malcolm Bradbury, I should not care to say in plain terms that it was a mistake. But it saves comparatively few words. It does nothing to ease comprehension: readers have to wait before they can discover who the bearer of all these attributes is. (To that extent it resembles the well known 'man who' trope of American political rhetoric: 'I have the honour to place in nomination the man who . . . the man who . . .', with the name held till the end.) And it is out of touch with the standard that authenticates good writing: normal speech. That is the device's real problem. Except satirically, you would never use it in talk.

Perhaps one day you will. Already I hear radio sports reporters using these piled-up attributes before a name— transferring to their broadcasting scripts a usage they learnt as newspapermen, and reading it aloud. ('Liverpool first-team forward-line acquisition Craig Johnston proved this after- noon . . .') It may catch on. But until it does, careful writers would still be wise to handle these things as they were handled, for example, by Addison, a founding father of my profession; who did not write (in *The Spectator* for 14 June 1711) that 'within the liberties of the city of Westminster lives fortyish, healthy-constitutioned, gay-tempered, elegant widow Lady Honoria', but preferred '. . . lives the Lady Honoria, a widow about the age of forty, of a healthy constitution, gay temper and elegant person'. At a cost of ten extra words, all of them short, he stayed speakable and instantly understandable.

The other kind of word that journalists like to put in front of a name to give information is a noun decribing a function. Often, when the noun of function is also a title, the practice works perfectly well: Professor Malcolm Bradbury; Bishop 'Wencher' Vlam (or even Bishop-Krakator, a special Slakan eminence); President Ronald Reagan. But it doesn't work with novelist Malcolm Bradbury, or vicar 'Wencher' Vlam, or prime minister Margaret Thatcher. Those prefixes are merely job-descriptions; they are not yet used in common speech as titles, and therefore—I submit—not ready to be used as such in good writing either.

So the shrewd course is to add one three-letter word to the description and comma the phrase off: 'Malcolm Bradbury, the novelist, describes . . .'; or 'the prime minister, Margaret Thatcher, calls . . .' Those commas mark the pauses you would observe in speech. And if you use that second word-order for a description that identifies your subject only generally rather than particularly, you don't need the commas: 'the novelist Malcolm Bradbury writes . . .'; because in speech you wouldn't need to pause.

It is true that habits of speech in this matter are different in the United States. There, descriptions of function are widely acceptable as titles; and the usage could well cross the Atlantic in time. Any day in Washington you can hear 'prime minister Thatcher'. Americans will do the same with 'Reverend'. When the assembly of the World Council of Churches met lately in Vancouver, I found myself in a broadcasting studio with an American minister named Oscar Macleod and the Archbishop

59

of Canterbury. Before the broadcast we had a word about how they were to be addressed. There was no difficulty in agreeing that the archbishop should be 'Archbishop' rather than 'your grace'. But the American asked to be addressed simply as 'Reverend'. A perceptible spasm of pain passed across the archbishop's face. 'Reverend', in American English, is a term grammatically on all fours with 'Archbishop': just as you can say 'Archbishop Robert Runcie', 'Archbishop Runcie', and 'Good morning, Archbishop', so in American English you can say 'Reverend Oscar Macleod', 'Reverend Macleod', and 'Good morning, Reverend.' In English English you can say none of those things and retain the good will of the clergy. 'Reverend' in English English is an adjective, just like 'Honourable' or 'Right Honourable'. You mayn't say 'Right Honourable Pym': you have to put a 'the' in front, and after 'Right Honourable' you have to put in 'Mr', or 'Francis', or both. And except in formal contexts you don't need to use it at all. Polite usage is exactly the same with 'Reverend'. (In fact the American turned out to have an honorary doctorate, so we settled for 'Dr Macleod', which sounded adequately pastoral.)

One other brevity beloved of journalists: to save a two-letter word out of 'Piccadilly, in London,' some of them will write 'London's Piccadilly'. But they would use that phrasing in speech only to trail a comparison they were about to make with Manchester's Piccadilly. Unless that is in fact their intention, they risk misleading their readers.

15
LEAVE THAT IN

The first religious experience that I can remember is getting under the nursery table to pray that the dancing mistress might be dead before we got to the dancing class. I was about half-way through the exasperating business which dancing class entailed: being changed right down to my skin, and washed and brushed, and having the comfortable dirt taken out of my fingernails. Margaret was sitting on the table, while Nana made her hair into long sausage-curls, with a wet brush round her finger. We thought the sausages very ugly, but Nana admired them, and we all loved Nana so much that we would do anything she liked.

Gwen Raverat, *Period Piece: A Cambridge Childhood*, Faber & Faber, 1952; chapter 11

A word often left out, for the sake of brevity or scansion, is the conjunction 'that'. 'They told me, Heraclitus, they told me you were dead'; or 'So high you can't get over it'.

Sometimes, as in both those instances, the shortened sentence remains clear. But not always. If Gwen Raverat had dropped the 'that' after 'pray' in her first sentence, she would have been left with 'to pray the dancing mistress', which readers might momentarily have understood as meaning 'to ask the dancing mistress'. Then the next words would have shown them they were on a wrong track, and they would have had to go back.

(I confess that, in the light of the thoughts on hyphenation which I set out in chapter 13, I should have preferred 'dancing-mistress' and 'dancing-class'. But I admit that these are borderline cases: the mistress, and the class, must have danced.)

Earlier in the book Gwen Raverat writes: 'I don't believe that my mother was more subject to attacks of theories than many other people of her time.' Drop that 'that', and you would be left with an opening five words suggesting at first glance a wholly unintended sense.

Similarly, dropping the 'that' after a 'so' can leave you with what looks for a moment like two separate sentences banged together without punctuation in between: 'we all loved Nana so much we would do anything she liked.'

'That' has another use: as a relative pronoun—'the first religious experience that I can remember'. This 'that', too, can be left out, at a certain risk to immediate intelligibility. But the more interesting question (though a difficult one to follow, I'm afraid) about 'that' in its relative sense is whether it is freely replaceable by 'which'. Gwen Raverat thinks it is. So do I. 'The first religious experience *that* I can remember', 'the exasperating business *which* dancing class entailed': the cases are identical. Both those relative clauses are of the kind called essential or restrictive (as already encountered in chapter 8). They give information that defines or identifies the noun (the experience, the business); and they work perfectly well with either 'that' or 'which'.

But there is another kind of relative clause: non-essential, or non-restrictive. It works only with 'which'. Gwen Raverat goes on to relate that she used to ask God to put 'chocolate pudding into the head of the cook, when she had intended to make marmalade pudding, which I hated'. Those last three words add important information, but not of an identifying kind; and 'that I hated' wouldn't do.

So because non-essential relative clauses need 'which', people of a tidy mind have often suggested that essential ones ought to be introduced only by 'that', to keep them distinct. It looks a neat idea, but it falls down on a number of counts.

First, it denies you the flexibility you need if you are to be read with ease. It would demand a 'that' in a sentence like 'The paper published the statement that the government had earlier released', because 'that the government had earlier released' is an essential clause, restricting your meaning to one statement and no other. But a 'that' leaves your reader for a moment in genuine doubt: instead of the relative 'that' it could just as well be the conjunctive 'that', introducing the substance of the statement—'that the government had earlier released three prisoners', for example. A 'which' would have forestalled that doubt. Freedom to use 'which' in such clauses also allows you to avoid using 'that' in two different senses in rapid succession, which can give the reader a slight jar: there is a 'which' to show what I mean in the bracketed paragraph which lies third in this chapter.

Second, any such principle—only 'that' for essential relative clauses, to mark them off from non-essential—is needless, because the real distinguishing mark is the timing, and therefore the punctuation. There are two relative clauses in the last sentence of the paragraph before this one. The first of them, 'which can give the reader a slight jar', is non-essential. But you hardly need to ask yourself grammatical questions about it: in speech you would pause before it, in writing you therefore put a comma before it, and that is the one distinguishing mark it needs. (It must have a comma at its other end, too, if it's not at the end of a sentence.) The second relative clause, 'which lies third in this chapter', is essential. It identifies the paragraph in

63

question. Again, you can hear the difference: in speech you would not pause before it, and so it takes no comma.

(In that second instance, but not in the first, I could equally well have used 'that'. If you have absolutely no ear, you can distinguish between the two kinds of relative clause in another way: where 'which' or 'who' can't be replaced by 'that', you need the comma.)

Third, and conclusively, the distinction fails the test of usage. Many good writers have known nothing of it. In her *John Ruskin* (1900), Alice Meynell throws off this remarkable parenthesis: 'Ruskin, at this time and ever after, used "which" where "that" would be both more correct and less inelegant. He probably had the habit from him who did more than any other to disorganize the English language—that is, Gibbon.' Even at the time, the passage provoked gentle ridicule; and it demonstrates exactly the opposite of what Mrs Meynell wanted to demonstrate. She is right about Gibbon's use of 'which': without searching far, I find him (in *The Decline and Fall of the Roman Empire*, 1776) writing of Constantinople harbour: 'The curve which it describes . . .' Alice Meynell is a capable writer of prose, but not in the class of Gibbon or Ruskin. Their authority overturns her point.

In passages which I chose for other reasons, from Shakespeare (published in about 1596 and quoted in chapter 17), Macaulay (1842, chapter 27), Lytton Strachey (1918, chapter 22), Wodehouse (1934, chapter 28), Alison Lurie (1974, chapter 31) and John Keegan (1982, chapter 11), I come upon the same use of 'which' to introduce essential relative clauses. The notion that this use is impermissible is a clear example of an imaginary rule which has no force. We shall meet others.

16
PARALLELOGRAMS

Old-fashioned moralists like to imagine communes as perpetually fragmented by conflict. Fragmented they may be, but more by drift than by explosion. People just move on. After all, there is nothing to keep them in one place rather than another, no compelling reason to continue loving one person rather than another. Shallowness hardens into indifference. In the last analysis nothing matters because everything is the same. It is the tragedy of the fraternal ideal that the longing for a fuller life should so often finish in emptiness, and that what began in enthusiasm should end in apathy.

Ferdinand Mount, *The Subversive Family*, Jonathan Cape, 1982; chapter 11

Stringing parallel phrases together can be pleasing to the reader; but it can also be confusing, if you leave out too much. This chapter, like the last, may seem hard going; but the point it discusses is important.

Consider our text from Ferdinand Mount, a writer who likes parallels and antitheses. He repeats the preposition 'by' in 'more by drift than by explosion', but he leaves out the second 'in' from 'in one place rather than another' (because he's going to echo 'rather than another' in a moment). Perfectly all right, both times. In each sentence, he provides two parallel parts.

The first time, the reader's path forks briefly before the preposition; the second time, after it; and 'than', or 'rather than', is the signal to the reader to pick up the sense again from the fork and discover the second half of the parallel.

(You don't always need a signal-word: Mount has another fork after 'there is', in his fourth sentence, and the reader returns to it for 'no compelling reason' without special sign.)

Yet even accomplished writers can trip, or allow their readers to. The second line of the Pope couplet that begins 'Hope springs eternal in the human breast', less well known than the first line, goes: 'Man never is, but always to be, blest.' (It comes from the *Essay on Man*, 1732–4.) Much is permitted to a poet; but, on a strict analysis, that second line doesn't work. The fork comes after 'Man'; the signal-word is 'but'. Yet the two parts aren't parallel: there's no verb in the second part. What Pope would have done better to write (I blush to correct so great a craftsman) is '. . . but e'er is to be'. 'Always' is a whole lot nearer common speech, though, than 'e'er'; and Pope—whose ear for colloquial phrasing keeps him astonishingly modern, 250 years on—will have put colloquialism above strict logic.

Problems most commonly arise when you have a series not of two parallel parts but of three. If Mount had been pressed for space, he might have written: 'Fragmented they may be, but by drift, departure or indifference.' Fine: all three parts parallel. Or '. . . by drift, by departure or by indifference.' Again fine. Not so fine, though, if he had written '. . . by drift, departure or through indifference.' You would then need a 'by' before 'departure'. Otherwise readers would think the fork came after 'by', and then stumble when they encountered 'through'.

Another stumbling-block would be 'They are either fragmented by drift or by departure.' The 'either' announces that readers have already passed a fork. You need 'They are either fragmented by drift or dispersed by departure'; or, more simply, 'They are fragmented either by drift or by departure.'

66

What follows 'either' has to be paralleled by what follows 'or'.

Replace 'either ... or' in that last paragraph by 'both ... and', or 'not only ... but also', and the same advice applies. You need an accurate match between the words immediately following 'both' and the words immediately following 'and' ('both hearing them and asking them questions', Luke 2:46, Authorized Version, 1611); or between the words immediately following 'not only' and the words immediately following 'but also'.

Once the stumbling-blocks are cleared away, parallelism gives pleasure; and for the same reason, I suppose, that symmetry gives pleasure. Parallelism is neat, craftsmanlike. It is also a prose equivalent of rhyme, and has something of the same trick of appealing to the reader's mind and lodging there. When thought is parallel, construction should be parallel: maxim and example in one.

Parallel constructions, as we saw at the start of this chapter, often leave a word or two to be supplied or understood by the reader from what has gone before: 'there is nothing to keep them in one place rather than another, (there is) no compelling reason to continue loving one person rather than another.' When that happens, parallelism has the extra virtue of being economical, both of space and of the reader's time. But words need not be left out in that way. The parallel clauses can be complete, and simply arranged one after the other with a conjunction, or a mark of punctuation, in between: 'nothing matters because everything is the same'.

With or without omissions, parallelism belongs particularly to that balanced century, the 18th. Examples are so numerous as to be hard to choose from. Here is Gibbon describing the end of an affair his father discountenanced: 'I sighed as a lover, I obeyed as a son' (*Memoirs*, published posthumously in about 1797). Or Pope on Addison: 'Willing to wound, and yet afraid to strike' (*Epistle to Dr Arbuthnot*, 1735). Or Gilbert Burnet,

67

who served William III, on the Buckingham who served Charles II: 'He was true to nothing, for he was not true to himself' (*History of His Own Time*, 1724).

But parallelism is older than the 18th century. Here is Dryden's mordant line on the same Buckingham and the men who beggared him: 'He had his jest, and they had his estate' (*Absalom and Achitophel*, 1681). And the great place to find parallels is the psalter of the 1662 Book of Common Prayer, a version of the Psalms first published by Coverdale in 1540. 'They that sow in tears: shall reap in joy' (126:6). 'Cast forth thy lightning, and tear them: shoot out thine arrows, and consume them' (144:6).

As distinct from all that, there is an intriguing figure of speech called chiasmus, where the two parallel lines are crossed into the shape of the Greek letter chi, which looks like a capital X. In the first part, B follows A: A follows B in the second part (thus). You can find that in the Psalms too. 'Give *the king thy judgments*, O God: and *thy righteousness* unto *the king's son*' (72:1). Not to be over-used: just an occasional, decorative variant.

17
RULES THAT AREN'T RULES

'What job is it, by the way? The one he's given you?'
'The one Bertram thought he was going to get.'

Christine began laughing noisily and blushing at the same time.
Dixon laughed too. He thought what a pity it was that all his faces
were designed to express rage or loathing. Now that something had
happened which really deserved a face, he'd none to celebrate it with.
As a kind of token, he made his Sex Life in Ancient Rome face.

Kingsley Amis, *Lucky Jim*, Gollancz, 1954; chapter 25

The great mistake is to interrupt your reader's willing concentration. That lays on you two duties. The first, which we have
been examining in the past six chapters, is to make yourself
understood at once. The second and related duty is to give no
avoidable offence. Good writing is to that extent a matter of
shrewd courtesy. It is those two obligations taken together
which constitute the practical reason for keeping the rules, by
which I mean those maxims or conventions about writing that
are deducible from good modern usage. (The two obligations
are also the reason for spelling by the book, however irrational
English practice may seem; and therefore for feeling satisfac-
tion, not shame, every time you consult a dictionary.)

But before we come on to maxims that deserve respect, it's worth clearing out of the way a few that don't. Many readers have been equipped, by some early influence on them, with a handful of precepts about writing which are defensible and helpful as long as they are seen for what they are: advice to the beginner. A few readers carry them through life as unbreakable commands. It is a pity to offend any reader; yet there are some such precepts you will sometimes have to neglect if your writing is not to become stilted, untrue to its author. Courtesy must yield to integrity.

Soon after these essays began to appear in their first form, two things I was reproached for by a handful of readers were allowing myself elisions ('it's', 'don't') and thinking a preposition a fit word to end a sentence or a phrase with. I take the response of those readers to be a sign that there are other readers like them, and that, in contexts calling for caution (like exams), elisions and tail-end prepositions should be used sparingly.

Both reproaches have a highly respectable ancestry. Swift objected to elisions (in *The Tatler* for 26 September 1710); Dryden combed tail-end prepositions out of the first-edition prefaces to his plays (republished in 1701, just after his death). The basic argument both men used was the same: that the usages were unknown in Latin and Greek; which is more or less true, and perfectly uncompelling, since we are not writing Latin or Greek.

The two usages were in fact well established in first-class writing long before Dryden and Swift, and have survived the disapproval of those eminent men serenely. Elisions abound in Shakespeare ('There's not the smallest orb which thou beholdest . . .'—*The Merchant of Venice, c.* 1596); in 17th-century sermons and essays ('But this, you'll say, is work only for the learned'—Cowley's *Several Discourses*, 1668); in relaxed 18th-century writers like Sterne ('That's pitiful beyond description'—*Tristram Shandy*, 1759); in the passages where

70

Thackeray addresses his reader direct ('I can't find ten saints in the list'—*Pendennis*, 1848-50).

Granted, those are examples from a conversational style of writing, which you won't always find appropriate. Granted, too, it is possible to write conversationally without elisions, as the Shaw passage showed in chapter 5. But to say that you needn't elide is a long way from saying that you mustn't elide.

Tail-end prepositions have a pedigree at least as old. You can find them in Latimer ('The king must appoint him sufficient to live upon; for I think verily there are a great many, which if the minister should have no living but at their appointment, he should not have clouting leather to piece his shoes with'—a passage about the parish clergyman from a sermon at Stamford in 1550); in the 1662 Book of Common Prayer ('. . .all such good works as thou hast prepared for us to walk in'); in Fielding ('The lady too plainly perceived that her waiting-gentlewoman knew more than she would willingly have had her acquainted with'—*Joseph Andrews*, 1742); in Hazlitt ('there is nothing that requires more precision, and, if I may so say, purity of expression, than the style I am speaking of'—'On Familiar Style', from *Table Talk*, 1821).

You may not wish to go as far as the nurse in the old joke who said to her charge: 'What did you choose that book to be read to out of for?' But for brevity, clarity or rhythm you may sometimes want to end with a preposition, and you need not be intimidated by any feeling that you are out of line with good writers.

Now look back at our text from Kingsley Amis, at a climactic point in a novel that set a pattern. 'He'd none to celebrate it with.' Crisp, apt, not to be faulted.

Another non-rule concerns the adjective 'like'. Six years after *Lucky Jim*, Amis brought out a novel called *Take a Girl Like You*. There are fusspots who want that kind of 'like' invariably changed to 'such as'. Yet competent writers have used the word

71

that way for years; and Penelope Mortimer, in her 1983 novel *The Handyman*, has '. . . single women like Lady Brabington or Miss Skeffington-Nodes'. The sanction of educated usage is still there.

That non-rule may have been put about by teachers who wanted to discourage the use of 'like' in general, because there are difficulties you can fall into with 'like' as a conjunction. Darwin wrote in an 1866 letter: 'Unfortunately few have observed like you have done'. *The Oxford English Dictionary*, which quotes that, says the usage is 'now generally condemned as vulgar or slovenly'. That is true. There are no good reasons for the condemnation, but it is a fact, and it is reason enough to rewrite: the accepted form is either 'as you have done' or 'like you'. Another usage similarly condemned, though pardoned in colloquial American, is 'like' for 'as if': 'He looks like he's asleep', sings the hero of *Oklahoma!* (1943). But the Amis, adjectival, use of 'like' is impeccable.

18
NUMBER AND GENDER

If a man should do something wrong, my brothers, on a sudden impulse, you who are endowed with the Spirit must set him right again very gently. Look to yourself, each one of you: you may be tempted too. Help one another to carry these heavy loads, and in this way you will fulfil the law of Christ.

For if a man imagines himself to be somebody, when he is nothing, he is deluding himself: then he can measure his own achievement by comparing himself with himself and not with anyone else. For everyone has his own proper burden to bear.

When anyone is under instruction in the faith, he should give his teacher a share of all good things he has.

Make no mistake about this: God is not to be fooled; a man reaps what he sows.

Galatians 6:1–7, New English Bible, 2nd edition, 1970

An iron convention, on the face of it, is that singular subjects take singular verbs and pronouns, whereas plural take plural. A man reaps what he sows; men reap what they sow. English is very lightly inflected as languages go, but that does seem to be one form of inflection it retains.

Yet I wonder whether even here it isn't a little difficult to talk of rules. I'm not just thinking of the exceptions: plural nouns that are now taken as singular ('Politics is a game'), or singular nouns that can still be treated as plural (like 'porridge': 'They're gude parritch eneugh', says a character in Scott's 1816 novel *Old Mortality*, and the usage is not dead in Scotland), or collective nouns that can be plural or singular according to whether the group is considered as a number of units or a whole ('Arsenal are all over the place. The crowd roars'). I'm thinking of words like everyone, anyone, someone, nobody and so on.

We shall go on writing, as the New English Bible does here, 'Everyone has . . .' But shall we go on writing 'Everyone has his . . .'? Lots of people say 'their'; and it has respectable precedents in writing. Jane Austen wrote in 1814, of the mixed theatricals at Mansfield Park: 'Everybody began to have their vexation.' I fancy we may see more of it. It flouts logic, but it solves an increasing problem.

The logic is clear enough. One is one and all alone and evermore shall be so; it is as singular as you can get; so its compound forms are singular too. A reader ingeniously suggested to me that we could regard 'everyone' as singular and 'everybody' as plural; but I doubt if it would catch on. Most people treat the two forms as interchangeable. The problem is that the meaning of 'his' has narrowed.

Till about the early 1970s, women—who preponderate in church—could listen to St Paul's words about men and take them to be about women too (whether or not Paul himself did). 'His' meant 'his or her'. Man embraced woman, as the grammarians used to say with a smirk.

No longer. Because of a slow revolution in states of mind among and about women, to a great many readers—male as well as female—'his' now means only 'his', not 'his or her'.

You can write 'his or her', but it's clumsy. Sometimes you can rephrase: 'People all have their . . .', 'We all have our . . .', 'You all have your . . .' Maybe that's the best that can be done for the moment. Educated opinion doesn't seem ready for the Jane Austen pattern: when I once wrote 'No one can afford to leave their written work untidy', several readers protested at the usage. Its time will come, I think, but can't be hurried. For the moment, we should be wise to write such sentences another way.

The problem is not so difficult to solve in a passage like this: 'Enormous blocks of print look formidable to a reader. He has a certain reluctance to tackle them; he can lose his way in them.' I find those sentences (where 'he' and 'his' must cover the female as well as the male reader) in the 1972 edition of E. B. White's revision of a generally admirable American booklet, nearly all of it applicable to English English, William Strunk's *The Elements of Style*. With a double change in number to prevent confusion, that could easily become: 'An enormous block of print looks formidable to readers. They have a certain reluctance to tackle it: they can lose their way in it.' Perhaps in some later edition the job has already been done.

Although the Strunk and White guide seeks to relieve them of it, many Americans impose on themselves an extra difficulty which the speaker and writer of English English is spared. They don't like the word 'one's'. Instead of 'One takes one's chance', they say—or they used to say—'One takes his chance.' But now they may well feel obliged to say 'One takes his or her chance', which is so laborious as to drive them either to readopt 'one's' or to rephrase the sentence.

Those are problems of number as well as gender. A related problem of gender, notoriously, applies to words like 'chairman' or 'actor' in contexts where they are meant to be common—of either gender. The problem is that they may not be understood as common; or that writers themselves may start off meaning them to be common, but then be drawn by the masculine form of the word into writing mainly about men.

The difficulty can be overcome. Some of these nouns are

75

already common: writer, reader, lawyer. Some have largely become common, losing their feminine form: editor, sculptor, poet. Some have an acceptable common alternative: player for actor, minister or cleric for clergyman. For the awkward remainder, like 'chairman', new forms like 'chairperson' have their support; but they come up against the slight overtone of ridicule or contempt that 'person' carries. ('Who is that young person whose hand my nephew Algernon is holding?'—Lady Bracknell, in Wilde's *The Importance of Being Earnest*, 1895.) An American experiment, 'chair-one', looks doomed; the Labour party's variant, plain 'chair'—'she is the chair of the housing committee'—looks silly. The awkwardness can easily be written round: 'she takes the chair at...', 'she chairs...' And you have brought in active verbs.

19
SPARING THE READER PAIN

'You plan to leave the Friday before Labor Day, and have your bus tickets, I understand. That'll get you home in time to get ready for school. Anthony, my dear, foolish, bright, crazy, lazy beamish boy, how I shall love and hate to see your back.'

'Would you like me to leave sooner? Do you object to me staying till then?'

'Object to *my* staying. The subject of a gerund is modified in the possessive,' she said, and burst into tears.

Watching her run out the back door and into the yard, I knew that my following her would have been not only useless, but inexcusable. I knew now and for all time what we meant and would mean to each other. But trying to comfort her as she wandered among the last of the summer flowers, my heart wrung like a dishcloth, would have served no purpose for either of us.

Peter De Vries, *Slouching Towards Kalamazoo*, Gollancz, 1983; chapter 10

No question, there are conventions of writing it is wise to abide by; and to them we now turn. Many of them can be taken as read among readers of this book: that most sentences begin with a capital letter and end with a full stop, or that a direct question finishes with a question-mark.

Some of these conventions, though, are worth dwelling on for one quality in particular: the extent to which breaching them can give the reader pain—disproportionate pain, maybe, but pain that need not be inflicted at all. And why risk having your reader burst into tears and run away, like Peter De Vries's schoolmistress-heroine Maggie Doubloon, when with a little tact you can avoid the rupture?

I take three examples. The first is the possessive-with-gerund convention: 'my staying'. Gerunds arouse passions. 'Save the gerund and screw the whale', says a character in Tom Stoppard's 1982 play *The Real Thing*.

Many of De Vries's jokes are about words and writing; and since in *Slouching Towards Kalamazoo* Miss Doubloon is not only with child by the young narrator but also his English teacher, the novel sometimes reads like a textbook of grammar cast in fictional form. 'Staying', in our passage here, is a gerund, a verbal noun. You could substitute an ordinary noun, like 'presence'. But you can't say 'me presence': you are well advised, therefore, not to say 'me staying'. And De Vries illustrates the point again with 'my following', which works as if it were 'my pursuit of'; and then he shows off a gerund without a possessive, in 'trying to comfort her'—a phrase which functions as the subject of the verb 'would have served' just as if 'trying to comfort her' were a noun like 'condolence'.

To tease the interested reader, De Vries also brings in an -ing word which is not a gerund but a participle, a verbal adjective: 'watching'. He uses it unexceptionably, to agree with the subject of the sentence, which is 'I'. If it did not—if he had written 'Watching her run into the yard, the thought of following her seemed...'—it would have been a dangling participle, suspended without a subject to hold on to. The dangling participle is the second of my red rags to concerned readers.

Participles have dangled for a long time. I have even found

one in *Gulliver's Travels* (1726), where Swift allows Gulliver, tied down by the Lilliputians, to say: 'I fell a-groaning with grief and pain; and then striving again to get loose, they discharged another volley larger than the first.' The subject of the first sentence, as far as the semicolon, is again 'I'. 'Striving', at the beginning of the second sentence, clearly describes the same character, and the reader expects the subject of this sentence to be the same. Instead it turns out to be 'they'. 'Striving' is left agreeing with nothing—dangling; and readers feel as if they too had missed a step, because their reasonable expectations have been disappointed.

A participle may legitimately stand free of either the subject or the object in a sentence if it has a noun of its own to agree with. In De Vries's 'my heart wrung like a dishcloth', 'wrung' is just such an instance. There is a plainer example still in John Mortimer's autobiography, *Clinging to the Wreckage* (1982): 'My Uncle Harold having died, my Aunt Daisy arrived with her dog and her shrubs to stay with my parents.' Mortimer had been put through the classical mangle at Harrow, as he describes; and any student of Latin would recognize 'My Uncle Harold having died' as a direct descendant of that old friend, the ablative absolute (absolute in the sense of free-standing). It goes straight in: *avunculo Haroldo mortuo*. Caesar's *Gallic War* is full of the same thing, except that the dead are seldom in the singular.

My third occasion of pain is the split infinitive. If instead of 'to comfort her', in the last sentence of our text, De Vries had written 'to properly comfort her', that would have been a split infinitive. Here the case is different from my two previous examples. There is no sound argument against split infinitives from grammar or logic. Nevertheless, there is an argument from usage and an argument from tact. The argument from usage is that split infinitives are rare in good writing. Shaw was a famous scourge of scourges of the split infinitive; but he did not

79

in fact split many himself. His reason may have been the other argument, from tact: that split infinitives do set many readers' teeth on edge. Schoolroom superstition it may be, but it is a curiously durable one. Many readers have a former English teacher in their lives, and one who liked infinitives unsplit. Better to leave that ghost unsummoned and the reader's attention undisturbed.

The same tact need not prevent the splitting of compound verbs. 'I had never wanted children', says Miss Doubloon half a page earlier. That 'never' intervenes between an auxiliary and its main verb; and a few enemies of liberty believe it ought not. Yet to displace it ('I never had wanted children') would be to ruin the natural rhythm. Perhaps because of the impossibility of unscrambling 'There'll always be an England', principled non-splitters of this type are chiefly found in the United States. The fact that De Vries, one of America's most literate writers, is not among them seems to me sufficient evidence that they are misguided.

20
DOUBLE-EDGED WORDS

And be these juggling fiends no more believ'd
That palter with us in a double sense;
That keep the word of promise to our ear,
And break it to our hope. I'll not fight with thee.

William Shakespeare, *Macbeth* (*c.* 1606); act V, scene vii

A different kind of text—an exhortation, not an example—
introduces a new suggestion about an old problem: the problem
of words used by large numbers of people in a sense which
linguistic purists disallow.

Purists can be tiresomely inconsistent. Macbeth's anger at
the witches is understandable. The apparitions they conjured
up in the fourth act told him that 'none of woman born/Shall
harm Macbeth', and that 'Macbeth shall never vanquish'd be
until/Great Birnam wood to high Dunsinane hill/Shall come
against him.' Then in the last act he realizes that, after they
have allowed the phrase 'Birnam wood' to be laxly interpreted
(as meaning merely branches from it carried by Malcolm's
army), they have turned purist over the word 'born': they are
using it only of normal delivery, and not of Caesarean section

81

(which produced Macduff, who now confronts Macbeth). Nevertheless, linguistic purists are a fact of life, and a necessary one. Usage is changing language all the time: the process might become headlong without whistleblowers. Give a word an altered meaning and, whatever you gain, you risk losing the old meaning; and there may be no satisfactory replacement.

The problem arises with those words where a shift in meaning is clearly in process but incomplete. The shift can take several decades. These words palter with us in a double sense; and they are a puzzle for the careful writer. Use them in the old sense, and readers who know them only in the new will be misled. Use them in their new sense, though, and readers who first learnt them in the old may be irritated; sometimes so sharply irritated that they will read no further.

The peaceable solution I offer is that you should give such words up altogether. It no longer helps to say combatively that their proper meaning is this or that. Change has gone too far. A word's meaning is what people take it to be; and over certain words people are divided. The safe and inoffensive course is to leave such words out of your vocabulary, as far as possible, until they can be said to have a single meaning again: until the new sense has either passed out of fashion or become established to the exclusion of the old.

Nine such vexed words may stand as examples. In the absence of a passage that uses them all, I have to make one up. Think of it as coming from a local newspaper's account of an old people's party.

Geriatric protagonists of contemporary verse were asked (unless disinterested in competing) to take a hopefully pristine sheet of paper, write a limerick on it, and hand it to the prestigious judge, whose reading of the winning items was arguably the most hilarious event of the evening.

82

The nine words are there all used in their new sense. Yet their old is in most cases still vigorous.

geriatric is an early-20th-century coinage from Greek words for 'old man' and 'doctor', and retains the meaning 'to do with treating the elderly'. (I owe most of these datings to the *Oxford English Dictionary* and its supplements.) But it is now also much used to mean simply 'elderly' or 'old person'.

protagonist was the Greek term for the first or chief actor in a drama (*protos agonistes*). But by association with 'antagonist' (*anti-agonistes*) it has often been taken in the past fifty years to mean 'defender', as if the prefix were the Latin 'pro'.

contemporary still bears its Latin meaning: 'of the same time'. Keith Thomas, writing in *Man and the Natural World* (1983) about the 17th century, says 'Contemporary horses differed in social nuance as much as do motor-cars today.' But the word has also been used all this century to mean 'of the same time as us', or 'present-day'. (Backers of this second sense take the word as meaning something more up-to-date than merely 'modern': after all, the *New Cambridge Modern History* (1957) begins at the Reformation.) Sometimes there is no telling which sense the writer intends.

disinterested means 'impartial'; having no pecuniary interest. But it is also increasingly used as a synonym for 'uninterested'.

hopefully used to mean only 'in hope': 'To travel hopefully is better than to arrive.' For half a century it has also been used to mean 'It is to be hoped': 'Hopefully we shall travel in comfort.' The usage is both convenient and defensible: comparable adverbs are used in that way without giving pain. ('Mercifully I was in time to buy the last four kilos': Dervla Murphy, of alfalfa for her mule, in *Eight Feet in the Andes*, 1983.) Yet nothing so affronts the purists. The word is not worth the hassle.

pristine has long meant 'former' (from Latin): Anthony How-ard, writing in the *Observer* for 12 February 1984, says that an earldom for Sir Alec Douglas-Home after his leaving office—he had been an earl before—would simply have been 'a return to his pristine status'. But through the influence of phrases like 'pristine whiteness', the word came at the turn of the century to be also understood as meaning 'unspoilt', 'mint-condition'.

prestigious comes from the Latin *prestigium*, which meant a trick; and the *OED* supplement quotes a use of the adjective as late as 1974, from the *Times Literary Supplement* in the days when its contributors were anonymous, to mean 'deceitful' (of a Lloyd George balancing act). The new sense, 'distinguished' ('pres-tigeful'), is dominant but not yet victorious.

arguably used to mean only 'disputably'. Lately it has been much used to mean 'perhaps', or even 'probably'. 'This is arguably the first . . .' is taken to mean not that there is a case against the claim but that there is a case in favour of it.

hilarious comes from a word found in both Greek and Latin meaning 'cheerful', 'merry', and has long borne that sense in English. Since about 1970 it has also served as a strong word for 'amusing': not showing merriment, but arousing it.

  In dictionaries not recently revised, a synonym often given for 'hilarious' is 'gay'—a notable example of a word that circumspect writers have largely abandoned, yet not necessarily for ever: its secondary sense may well yield in due time to a fresh euphemism, and the word's original sense of 'cheerful' be unmistakable again. But these movements of language can't be rushed; and until a shifting word settles down, prudence counsels renunciation.

III MAKING THE DIFFERENCE

21
THE RICHES OF RHYTHM

Almost directly underneath us was the greatest of Mlanje's many dark gorges, the Great Ruo Gorge. The water of the Great Ruo itself plunged down the top end of the gorge; fell with a wild, desperate, foaming leap into an abyss, thousands of feet deep. We could not see the bottom of it. On either side it was flanked by black, glistening, six-thousand-foot cliffs, tapering off into grey peaks nine thousand feet high. The whole of the gorge rustled, whispered, and murmured with the sound of falling water, which at every change of mountain air would suddenly break over us with a noise like the sound of an approaching hail-storm.

Laurens van der Post, *Venture to the Interior*, Hogarth Press, 1952; chapter 14

So far we have been considering how to sound like yourself, and how to be readily understood. Now we bring in a touch of artifice; starting with sound again, and moving on to pictures.

There is no writing without rhythm. The rhythm of written words in prose is the irregular sequence of stressed and unstressed syllables that the writer and the reader, guided by the sense and the punctuation, hear in their heads. The stress within individual words is not in question. In the word 'without', for example, the accent falls on the second syllable. But in the opening sentence of this paragraph most readers would leave that word unleant on, and stress only 'no' and the first syllables of 'writing' and 'rhythm'.

The natural unit of prose rhythm is even longer than the sentence: it's the paragraph. (I first met that observation, and the Gibbon quotation in my next paragraph, in the 1952 edition of Sir Herbert Read's *English Prose Style*.) For good writers, the paragraph is the span within which a single rhythm begins and ends, accompanied by variations in pace and in the pitch of the inner voice. Our passage from Sir Laurens van der Post is one whole paragraph. Besides stressing the appropriate syllable in 'directly', 'greatest' and so on, and pausing with the punctuation, the voice would speed up a little during the second sentence, drop in pitch at the end of that sentence and during the third, and—having risen again in pitch in the latter part of the fourth sentence—lose pace in the last.

Gibbon, a master of rhythm, claimed in his *Memoirs* (*c*. 1797) that he listened to a whole paragraph in his head before he wrote any of it down: 'It has been my practice to cast a long paragraph in a single mould, to try it by my ear, to deposit it in my memory, but to suspend the action of the pen till I had given the last polish to my work.'

All paragraphs have a rhythm of a kind. The test of a pleasing rhythm is whether a paragraph is speakable; and the judge, as Gibbon says, is your own ear. Your ear can be educated. In Bertrand Russell's *Autobiography* (1967) there is a dry anecdote about Lytton Strachey's mother: 'Lady Strachey was a woman of immense vigour, with a great desire that some at least of her children should distinguish themselves. She had an admirable sense of prose and used to read South's sermons aloud to her children, not for the matter (she was a free thinker) but to give them a sense of rhythm in the writing of English.' Robert South was a court preacher under Charles II. You can hear his form in this passage from a sermon at Oxford in 1668 about the proper maintenance of the clergy: 'I scarce ever knew any ecclesiastic but was treated with scorn and distance; and the only peculiar respect I have observed shown such persons in this nation (which yet I dare say they could willingly enough dispense with) is, that sometimes a clergyman of an hundred pound a year has the honour to be taxed equal to a layman of ten thousand.' Certainly Lytton Strachey did develop an acute ear for prose rhythm, as the quotation towards the end of my next chapter shows; and his rhythms (and for that matter Bertrand Russell's) can often give the reader the same feeling as South's, of a sharp mind with its edge tempered by amusement.

For rhythm can be apt as well as pleasing. Sometimes it can reinforce meaning and mood. In the Authorized Version of the Bible (1611), the relief and fatigue at the end of the shipwreck in Acts 27 are caught in the long, concluding syllables: 'And so it came to pass, that they escaped all safe to land.' The relaxed and cultivated tone of Sir Thomas Browne's speculations in *Urn Burial* (1658) is echoed in their cadences: 'Time, which antiquates antiquities, and hath an art to make dust of all things, hath yet spared these minor monuments.' In Cowper's letters, like this one to his cousin Lady Hesketh in 1785 about a visit from the doctor, you can hear the subdued music of domesticity: 'And lastly, I am to drink no wine at night, but, instead of my usual supper, am to regale myself with half a pint of oatmeal gruel, made very good with spice, and into which he graciously admits four table spoonfuls of brown port.' Ruskin, in *The Crown of Wild Olive* (1866), reproduces the clangour of urban life: 'So all that great foul city of London there—rattling, growling, smoking, stinking—a ghastly heap of fermenting brickwork, pouring out poison at every pore—you fancy it is a city of work? Not a street of it! It is a great city of play; very nasty play, and very hard play, but still play.' Stevenson, in *Virginibus Puerisque* (1881), on walking tours (favourite theme of essayists from Hazlitt to Levin), matches the beat of his words to his movements: 'And no sooner have you passed the straps over your shoulder than the lees of sleep are cleared from you, you pull yourself together with a shake, and fall at once into your stride.'

Van der Post, too, adapts the sound of his prose to the solemnity and menace of the surroundings he describes. A few pages on from our text he contrives a still closer bond between sound and sense, using rhythm to imitate a specific sound: 'It was as if the earth underneath my head was slowly beginning to respond to this drumming, this insistent beat of the rain; to take up this rhythm of the rain . . . Whenever I rose in the night to make up the fire there was the rain and this manner of the rain; and when I lay down again there was this deep, rhythmical response of the earth.'

But rhythm can do something more useful than influence mood. It can clarify meaning; as the next chapter shows.

22
PLACING THE EMPHASIS

He went into an Espresso bar and drank some coffee. No one turned round to look at him. He was a failure, certainly. Failure, it occurred to him, was the secular equivalent of sin. Modern secular man was born into a world whose moral framework was composed not of laws and duties, but of tests and comparisons. There were no absolute outside standards, so standards had to generate themselves from within, relativistically. One's natural sense of inadequacy could be kept at bay only by pious acts of repeated successfulness. And failure was more terrifying than sin.

Michael Frayn, *Towards the End of the Morning*, Collins, 1967; chapter 6

The vital thing about rhythm is that it governs emphasis. As you read through that passage of Michael Frayn (from a funny and truthful novel about journalists), listen to the emphases—the places where the rhythm imposes the principal stresses. You will notice something simple but important. Nearly all of them fall just before a pause, as marked by punctuation: at the end of sentences, or of subordinate parts of sentences. Apply that device, if you don't use it already, and it will do more than any other single change to make your writing tell.

It isn't automatic. End a sentence with weak words, and the

emphasis is driven forward; as in the second Frayn sentence, where it falls—by the writer's wish—on the word 'look'. But most commonly the main emphasis drops on to the word before the full stop. In the first Frayn sentence, it falls unmistakably on 'coffee'—and so solidly as to remove a problem about 'some', often an unsafe word because readers cannot immediately tell whether they are to hear it in its clipped pronunciation (the king's 'Give me some light' in *Hamlet*) or as a whole sound (the king's 'How some have been depos'd' in *Richard II*). Frayn clearly wants the former.

The emphasis goes to the end in more complicated sentences than that. Consider this marvellous sentence from that great newspaper novel, Evelyn Waugh's *Scoop* (1938): 'Mrs Earl Russell Jackson padded in stockinged feet across the bare boards of the lounge looking for a sizeable cigar-end, found one, screwed it into her pipe, and settled down in the office rocking-chair to read her Bible.'

Moreover, if you manoeuvre the words you want into positions of emphasis you will never need that telltale sign of the slack writer, the exclamation-mark at the end of an ordinary indicative sentence. Exclamation-marks are useful enough after exclamations or imperatives (Shelley's line 'O world! O life! O time!'; or Belloc's, as spoken by the keeper to the boy-eating lion, 'Let go, Sir! Down, Sir! Put it down!'). They can be defended even after indicative sentences if those sentences can claim the licence of dialogue as being reported thoughts. (In his 1875 novel *The Way We Live Now*, Trollope, a specialist in dialogue, has his fraudulent financier reflecting: 'The girl was his own daughter! The money had been his own money! The man had been his own servant!') But as a signal that you believe or hope you have just written something surprising or amusing, an exclamation-mark is calamitous. It amounts to a nudge in the ribs, a guffaw at your own joke. In that Waugh passage, the incongruity between Mrs Earl Russell Jackson's preparations and their outcome is made plain by the shape of the sentence. Suppose—disquieting thought—that Waugh had not been content with the emphasis bestowed on the word 'Bible' by its position, and had followed it with an exclamation-mark. At once, in place of professionalism, that part of the sentence would have shown the desperate jocularity of those duplicated letters sent out at Christmas-time by missionaries. Avoid missionary prose. Remember that a colloquialism for exclamation-mark is 'shriek-mark', and shriek as little as you can.

But besides the emphasis before a full stop, there are lesser emphases before lesser punctuation marks: in the Waugh sentence, on 'cigar' and 'found' and 'pipe'. And you can use this convenient fact to emphasize a word that is nowhere near the end of a sentence or a part of one. Look at 'Failure' in Frayn's fourth sentence. It suffers from a double weakness: it is at the very beginning of a sentence, and it repels stress because it is a repeat of a word we have just had. But Frayn's interpolation of 'it occurred to him' immediately afterwards, between commas, secures the pause that gives the emphasis he wants.

You can do the same thing with the smallest word, a 'so', a 'but'. Just to shove in a comma, though, lacks logic. You need an interpolation that takes commas at both ends—like this 'after all' from Lytton Strachey, at the famous close of his essay on Cardinal Manning in *Eminent Victorians* (1918): 'For whatever cause, the minds of the people had been impressed; and yet, after all, the impression was more acute than lasting. The Cardinal's memory is a dim thing today. And he who descends into the crypt of that Cathedral which Manning never lived to see, will observe, in the quiet niche with the sepulchral monument, that the dust lies thick on the strange, the incongruous, the almost impossible object which, with its elaborations of independent tassels, hangs down from the dim vault like some forlorn and forgotten trophy—the Hat.'

You very seldom need to read a Lytton Strachey sentence

twice: whether or not because of that childhood exposure to South's rhythmic sermons, he gets the pauses, and therefore the emphases, dead right. Yet on a great many people his example has been lost. A reader wrote to me lately: 'In the Grammar School I went to, we were taught never to punctuate before "and". A comma is needless before "and"; a semicolon makes "and" itself superfluous; a full stop before "and" is a sin!'

I find that a melancholy example of the way we make writing more difficult, for writer and reader, than it need be. I prefer the liberating example of writers like Lytton Strachey—and Waugh, you will notice, and Frayn, and countless others.

23
EMPHASIS BY REPETITION

I have a dream that one day on the red hills of Georgia the sons of former slaves and the sons of former slave-owners will be able to sit down together at the table of brotherhood. I have a dream that one day even the state of Mississippi, a state sweltering with the heat of oppression, will be transformed into an oasis of freedom and justice . . .

I have a dream that one day every valley shall be exalted, every hill and mountain shall be made low. The rough places will be made plain, and the crooked places will be made straight. This is the faith that I go back to the South with. With this faith we will be able to hew out of the mountains of despair the stone of hope. With this faith we will be able to work together, to pray together, to struggle together, to go to jail together, to stand up for freedom together, knowing we will be free one day.

Martin Luther King, speech to the march on Washington, 1963; from Kenneth Slack, *Martin Luther King*, SCM Press, 1970, chapter 4

The human ear enjoys repetition. At Greek island banquets nearly three thousand years ago, travelling reciters of Homer studded their text with *reprises* to gratify their guests; on the grassy spaces in Washington in front of the memorial to

President Lincoln, a quarter of a million people responded with rising fervour to Martin Luther King's iterated cry 'I have a dream'. In a speech composed with infinite art, making use of pictorialism, of the poetry in place-names, of variation in sentence-length, of metaphor, of quotation, this was the high point. 'Tell us!' the voices in the crowd called out. 'Dream some more'!'

But what they wanted to know, each time, was what the dream was; or, later, what could be achieved 'with this faith'. That is the point. In passages where words are repeated, the interest, and the emphasis, attaches to the new matter: the words that are not repeated.

(One of King's allusions was to the passage in the 11th chapter of the Epistle to the Hebrews where the writer begins 15 different paragraphs, in the Greek original as in the English translations, with the phrase 'By faith'; thus concentrating attention each time on the different things that past believers have done by faith. 'By faith Isaac blessed Jacob and Esau concerning things to come. By faith Jacob, when he was a dying, blessed both the sons of Joseph; and worshipped, leaning upon the top of his staff. By faith Joseph, when he died, made mention of the departing of the children of Israel; and gave commandment concerning his bones. By faith Moses, when he was born, was hid three months . . .' I quote from the Authorized Version.)

Lincoln himself had used the device at Gettysburg a hundred years before King: 'But, in a larger sense, we cannot dedicate, we cannot consecrate, we cannot hallow this ground.' Even for the reader, the chief stress falls unmistakably on 'consecrate' and 'hallow'.

Certainly it is a device of rhetoric, not suitable in all contexts; and the fact that, searching for modern instances, I found more American examples than English suggests to me that it may be more pleasing to the American than the English ear. But there is a form of the device that most of us use all the time. Repetition can place emphasis where it would not normally fall.

In the word 'slave-owners' the ordinary stress, as with most such composite nouns, falls on the word 'slave'. But King has just used the word 'slave'; and the inner ear dislikes stressing the same word twice in quick succession. The emphasis is therefore shifted to the word 'owners' as surely as if the writer had italicized it.

Indeed, the stratagems I have been setting out in this chapter and the one before it—emphasizing a word by repeating one next to it or by marking a pause just after it—are the chief means whereby careful writers contrive to use italics hardly at all. (The same goes for underlining, the equivalent of italics in typescript and manuscript.) Italics are occasionally unavoidable, to make sure a point is not lost. Yet without being as shrill as an exclamation-mark, italics have a quality of over-insistence. The reader's ear is attuned to fine gradations of emphasis: a word in italics is a sudden, disproportionate shout. And italics have other snags. On the page they draw the eye, and may divert the reader's attention. They are in common use for titles and foreign words: deploy them for emphasis in a piece of writing where they are already serving one of those other purposes, and you risk confusion. If you are writing for print, and your editor asks the printer to set the whole of your material in italics, your italics-for-emphasis will go for very little: the printer may reverse them into roman, but they will scarcely show. Italicize reluctantly.

The trick of emphasis-by-adjacent-repetition is especially useful at the ends of clauses and sentences, where emphasis most readily falls—before the pauses marked by punctuation. If the last word or phrase is a repeated word or phrase, the emphasis is thrown forward (as on to that word 'repeated'). Lincoln did it in the last sentence of his Gettysburg address with 'government of the people, by the people, for the people', to call attention to those unpromising prepositions 'by' and 'for'. King does it to emphasize that string of infinitives after 'to work'.

Most often, though, the device is used not in multiple repetition but in simple. It is at least as old as Shakespeare. 'We fail!' exclaims Lady Macbeth to her husband (when he suggests that, in the attempt to murder Duncan, that might happen): 'But screw your courage to the sticking-place,/And we'll not fail.' Impossible to read those lines, or say them, without leaning on the 'not'. A device which will do that for you is a good device.

24
SHORT WORDS AND LONG

He swam a little farther out and then dived again so that he went vertically down to where the ramp ended and then swam out along the soft lake floor. He opened his eyes, but now there was nothing to be seen except an obscure green light. Fascinated, he clove the very soft ooze with his hands as he glided along. It was so soft, almost as soft and giving as the water, and yet somehow sinister. Supposing he were to find a corpse or something, a human form half buried in that deep ancient deposit? As he thought this thought Toby's hand encountered something hard and rough.

Iris Murdoch, *The Bell*, Chatto & Windus, 1958; chapter 10

It is an old saw that you do well to use short words: words of one or at most two syllables. Short words oblige clear thought, keep you from showing off, are taken on board by most readers and save space. Pundits on style used above all to like short words that came from Anglo-Saxon rather than Latin roots, as if Anglo-Saxon spoke with a special voice to the English-speaking soul; but there are plenty of good short words from Latin too: lake, corpse, human; move, pure, oil, image.

The old saw is mainly right. Yet you can't stay away from long words all the time, short of childish circumlocution.

'Circumlocution' is itself a word that would need several other words to fill its place; so sticking to short words wouldn't always keep you brief. More, it wouldn't make you easy to read. Sameness of any kind is after a while a bore. The odd long word among your short words saves you from that, and enjoys besides a certain emphasis.

Iris Murdoch's story about the break-up of a religious community in Gloucestershire is told with a plainness of phrase that borders on the childlike: witness the way the word 'then' comes twice in that first sentence. One effect the technique seems to me to have is to make the still, summer landscape as vivid to the reader's senses as it would be to a child's. The force that pulls the community apart is symbolized by a drowned bell, and the boy Toby's finding it is the hinge of the book. In such passages, the writer's regular and apt use of short words throws into relief those few longer words, ordinary in themselves, she now and then calls on: vertically, fascinated, sinister, deposit, encountered.

The value of contrast in word lengths was well known to the translators of the Authorized Version of the Bible (1611). In Judges (6:19), Gideon tests his standing with God by making an offering. 'The flesh he put in a basket, and he put the broth in a pot, and brought it out unto him under the oak, and presented it.' The sudden extra length of the word 'presented' catches the contrast between simple instruments and solemn manner. (The verse also illustrates chiasmus and—like our Iris Murdoch text—the use of active verbs.)

The same technique of contrast is used at a loftier level with the word 'everlasting' in a verse from Isaiah (60:19). 'The sun shall be no more thy light by day; neither for brightness shall the moon give light unto thee: but the Lord shall be unto thee an everlasting light, and thy God thy glory.'

A writer who may well have learnt variation of word-lengths from the Authorized Version is Newman. 'I was brought up from a child to take great delight in reading the Bible', he says in his *Apologia pro Vita Sua* (1864); and in the passage from the same book where he denies that the high-church movement at Oxford had been under his leadership, he allows important words to stand out from the rest simply by their greater length. 'My great principle ever was, live and let live. I never had the staidness or dignity necessary for a leader. To the last I never recognized the hold I had over young men. Of late years I have read and heard that they even imitated me in various ways. I was quite unconscious of it, and I think my immediate friends knew too well how disgusted I should be at the news, to have the heart to tell me.'

Another writer brought up on the Authorized Version, and versed in the effectiveness of varied word-lengths, was Buchan. Long words tell by their rarity in his account of Thomas Carlyle Craw, the Northcliffe/Rothermere/Beaverbrook figure in *Castle Gay* (1930): 'He realized that the way to fortune did not lie in writing for other men. He must own the paper which had its vogue from his talents, and draw to himself the whole profits of exploiting the public taste. Looking about him, he decided that there was room for a weekly journal at a popular price, which would make its appeal to the huge class of the aspiring half-baked, then being turned out by free education.'

The device can be reversed. Drop a few short words in among a mass of long ones, and it's the short ones that count. That works best for grandiloquent writers like Johnson. You can see it in this passage from 'An essay on the origin and importance of fugitive pieces' (1744): 'The multiplicity of religious sects tolerated among us, of which every one has found opponents and vindicators, is another source of unexhaustible publication, almost peculiar to ourselves; for controversies cannot be long continued, nor frequently revived, where an inquisitor has a right to shut up the disputants in dungeons.' In that press of long words, the phrase 'to shut up' takes on a calculated force.

Once grandiloquence began to be seen by most readers as having a hint of the absurd about it, that Johnsonian reversal of the Authorized Version's pattern became chiefly a device of comic writing. Dickens uses it a lot. In *David Copperfield* (1850) you can find: 'From this document I learned that Mr Micawber, being again arrested, was in a final paroxysm of despair; and that he begged me to send him his knife and pint pot, by bearer, as they might prove serviceable during the brief remainder of his existence in jail.' There 'knife', 'pint pot' and 'jail' push themselves on your notice like the pips in a grape, the grit of real life not to be disguised in a mush of fine phrases. But this is part of a running joke about Mr Micawber: his constant deflation of his own pomposity. That is not a service which in ordinary contexts the careful writer ought to need.

25
SHORT SENTENCES AND LONG

'Whose love has laid hold on us in Jesus.' Jesus is the image and likeness of God in human terms; he has done God's work in human space and time. Faced with this truth, I cannot stop there. I have to go beyond it to an even greater affirmation, because of the very nature of love. It is inconceivable to me that love could ever say: 'I must save these children of mine, and that will mean the most terrible suffering. I will find someone else to do the job.' Love does not send others to suffer in its place. Love comes itself.

John Austin Baker, *The Foolishness of God*, Darton, Longman & Todd, 1970; postscript

As with words, so with sentences. Short sentences are good; sentences of varied length are better. That kind of variety is attractive in itself, and lends emphasis to the exceptional, particularly if the exception is a short sentence among long ones. Within whole sentences you can further the variation by using colons and semicolons to make lesser sentences. John Austin Baker, the best prose writer in the Church of England ministry today and now Bishop of Salisbury, demonstrates that skill throughout his brave postscript.

It is a commonplace of advice about writing that you should

say what you have to say as briefly as possible. The maxim is in general sound, since brevity shows a wise concern for your reader; though it is not an especially helpful maxim, since it skips over the prior question, which is what do you have to say. The time to secure brevity, as we saw in chapter 3, is when you answer that question in order to make your plan before you write. Anything once written can be shortened, as the half-length Reader's Digest version of the Bible (1983) shows; yet not everything is improved by being shortened. If what you have to say is a narrative that depends for its persuasiveness on the accumulation of detail, or if it is an exhortation that needs the iterations of rhetoric, then the single-minded pursuit of brevity will do harm. The Baker passage would make sense without the words 'I cannot stop there.' But to lose them would be to lose something of the sense of a mind's wondering journey. Varying your sentence-lengths will cost you a few extra words: those extra words could sometimes be saved, for example, by turning a separate sentence into a relative clause. I could there have written: '. . . cost you a few extra words, which could sometimes . . .'; that would have saved two words. (I did not have the option of writing '. . . cost you a few extra words: they could sometimes . . .', because it would not have been immediately clear whether 'they' meant the extra words or the sentence-lengths.) But I would then have had one rambling sentence of 26 words instead of the tidy juxtaposition of one sentence of 10 words with another, slower-paced, of 18. And my reader would have been, by a hair's breadth, less willing than before to stay with me.

A specialist in varied sentence-lengths was Burke. Look at the famous passage from *Reflections on the Revolution in France* (1790) about Marie Antoinette: 'Little did I dream, when she added titles of veneration to those of enthusiastic, distant, respectful love, that she should ever be obliged to carry the sharp antidote against disgrace concealed in that bosom; little did I dream that I should have lived to see such disasters fallen upon her in a nation of gallant men, in a nation of men of honour, and of cavaliers. I thought ten thousand swords must have leapt from their scabbards to avenge even a look that threatened her with insult. But the age of chivalry is gone. That of sophisters, economists and calculators has succeeded...' And off he goes again. The seven-word sentence about chivalry derives hammer-like intensity from being preceded first by a very long sentence, in two parts, and then by a fairly long one.

Many writers have used a simplified variant, a long sentence followed by a short, as their opener. Chesterton begins an essay called 'Rabelaisian regrets' (in *The Common Man*, 1950) like this: 'There has arisen in our time an extraordinary notion that there is something humane, open-hearted or generous about refusing to define one's creed. Obviously the very opposite is the case.' It is a gambit worth borrowing.

Short sentences have many virtues. Like short words, they make for clear thought in the writer and easy understanding in the reader. The eye, and therefore the mind, can take them in all at once: that gives them peculiar penetration. Since short sentences mean more sentences, and emphasis falls at sentence-ends, short sentences mean more emphasis. And a succession of short sentences can create an air of action, excitement. 'She left the web, she left the loom, /She made three paces through the room, /She saw the water-lily bloom, /She saw the helmet and the plume, /She looked down to Camelot. /Out flew the web and floated wide...' Thus Tennyson, the supreme technician, in 'The Lady of Shalott' (1832), at the moment when the lady decides to break the house rules.

Much of the effort of varying your sentence-lengths, therefore, properly goes into carving out short sentences. But short sentences also have limitations. Being short, they seldom have room for subordinate clauses. That means they can seldom accommodate complex ideas. It also means that they can easily become monotonous, because they lack the occasion for changes of pace and pitch which subordinate clauses and their punctuation allow.

That problem is the same even if you join a few of your short sentences up with 'and'. You risk sounding like an imitation of Hemingway. 'There was much traffic on the roads and the drivers couldn't see where they were going. The traffic lights changed from red to amber to green and back to red again and the traffic didn't move. Then the drivers sounded their horns and got out of their cars to swear at each other. It was foggy in London that afternoon and the dark came very early.'

That is not real Hemingway, but an illuminating parody of Hemingway in David Lodge's novel *The British Museum is Falling Down* (1965). The book contains nine other parodies, including one of James and one of Joyce—long-sentence-men both; and its hero is a young academic who is doing a PhD thesis about 'the structure of long sentences in three modern English novels'. The book leaves you in no doubt that long sentences in the mass are as unreadable as short ones in the mass. But intersperse the two, and you begin to be readable.

26
SENTENCES INTO PARAGRAPHS

Whatever the lawyer was saying to her was arousing her to a terrifying pitch of fury. Her jowls shook. Her moustache bristled. 'Crooks!' she kept shouting. Otherwise she shouted in Punjabi. Then she banged the phone down, forced her immense body out of the cubby-hole and shouted, 'Fool! Fool!'

And pushed him.

Pushed him.

In full view of the servants.

The physical shock was great. The humiliation unbearable. 'Why do you push me?' he shouted at her as she waddled her way back to her room.

'Because you are a fool!' she shouted back . . .

Paul Scott, *Staying On*, William Heinemann, 1977; chapter 12

There was once an editor of the *Yorkshire Post* who decreed that every paragraph in the paper should have two sentences in it: no more, no fewer. He was obeyed, as all editors must be, but the decree was the negation of good writing. A paragraph is not a fixed shape, like a page. It works as words and sentences do: a small one among big ones draws the reader's special interest and attention. When Mr Bhoolabhoy (the hotel manager), from whose point of view the story is being told at that moment, is pushed by Mrs Bhoolabhoy (the hotel owner), the suddenness and outrage of the assault is much more sharply conveyed by Paul Scott's three very short paragraphs than it would have been by the adverbs 'suddenly' and 'outrageously'; and Mr Bhoolabhoy's inner scream is at its highest pitch in the middle paragraph of the three, where brevity is reinforced (justifiably, I think) with italics.

The example is an extreme one, chosen so as not to take up too much room. Paul Scott varies his paragraph-lengths a good deal: in a more typical passage, in chapter 9, the number of lines in half-a-dozen successive paragraphs is 12, 3, 10, 1, 8 and 25. (The calculation is from the 1978 Panther paperback.)

And paragraphs vary in length for another and more important reason than ornament or effect. A paragraph is a unit of thought. (That is why it is also a unit of rhythm, as we saw in chapter 21.) It should be, as a general rule, the elaboration of a single point. But you can't help having more to say about some points than others. So in properly thought-out prose, paragraph-length is bound to be uneven.

Sometimes you may feel a temptation to cram all your material on one point into a single sentence rather than a single paragraph. Reporters often yield to that temptation in the very first sentence of a story—the sentence which must tell the reader (and, before that, the news editor) that here is a piece which for interest and importance demands to be read. But the procedure has a breathlessness about it which can be self-defeating; and if you are delivered from the harshest imperatives of journalism, you will be wise if you let that first swollen sentence become instead a paragraph with two or three sentences in it.

Not that the occasional long sentence is a bad thing. But it is easiest for the reader to manage when it is a long sentence of a specialized kind, where everything that matters is set out at the beginning, and the rest is just a series of additions, all in the same form as each other, hooked on one after the other like railway-trucks behind an engine. There are several such sentences in Hemingway's apologetic epilogue to *Death in the Afternoon* (1932): 'Nor does it tell about Zaragossa, at night on the bridge watching the Ebro, and the parachute jumper next day and Rafael's cigars; nor the jota contests in the old red plush theatre and the wonderful boy and girl pairs; nor when they killed the Noy de Sucre in Barcelona, nor about any of that; nor...' And there is a much longer one, approaching 1700 words, in Bernard Levin's *Enthusiasms* (1983): 'No meal I have ever eaten could be truly compared to a performance of Schubert's *Death and the Maiden* quartet by the Amadeus on their finest form, not even *chez* Girardet in the suburbs of Lausanne, where they make a tea sorbet out of their own blend of Darjeeling and Earl Grey, nor *chez* Hure in Avallon, where Napoleon stopped on the way north...' You can keep that sort of thing up for ever.

A long sentence becomes awkward when you make your reader wait for an important element, like the main verb. Let me invent a specimen. 'The kind of long sentence built up partly from a list but also with any number of brackets or subordinate clauses hanging off it in swags can most easily be found in the rambling but mellifluous recollections of De Quincey.'

Many writers, having committed some such sentence to paper, and perceiving it to be a little hard on the reader's staying-power, are tempted to bang in a comma after 'swags'. But that kind of pause-for-breath comma has no more justification in logic than a comma has in a sentence like 'Long sentences, abound in De Quincey.' If you do put a comma after 'swags', you also need one after 'list', to turn that 'but also' phrase into an interpolation; or you could add a fresh interpolation after the new comma: '... in swags, like ripe fruit, can most easily be found...' Then you would at least be taking advantage of the principle that an interpolation carries punctuation at each end.

Far better, though, to turn the whole thing into a paragraph, with three or four sentences in it. 'A long sentence often starts life as a list. Then the writer hangs brackets and subordinate clauses on to the items in the list. You can find that kind of sentence . . .'

Paragraphs thus organized—a paragraph to a point, and never mind the length or lack of it—help your reader to see which thoughts go with which. Tabloid newspapers, and the kind of newspaper advertisement which contains a lot of text, regularly throw that advantage away by making every fresh sentence a fresh paragraph. This inhibits the writer from developing a point, and half-implies that the reader would be too lazy to follow the development anyway.

Newspapers, at any rate, and especially tabloids, do have special problems with the narrowness of most of their columns: it can turn a paragraph of more than a few sentences into a forbidding pillar of type. If you have the freedom to deploy your paragraphs on ordinary pages, use it gratefully and variously.

27
THE VIVID INSTANCE

It was his duty to praise, to look always beyond the facts to the official figures; for it was part of the *Sentinel's* new policy of sobriety that this was the best of all worlds and Trinidad's official institutions its most magnificent aspects. He had not so much to distort as to ignore: to forget the bare, toughened feet of the children in an orphanage, the sullen looks of dread, the shameful uniforms; to accept a temporary shaming eminence and walk through workshops and vegetable gardens, noting industry, rehabilitation and discipline; to have lemonade and a cigarette in the director's office, and get the figures; to put himself on the side of the grotesques.

V. S. Naipaul, *A House for Mr Biswas*, André Deutsch, 1961; part 2, chapter 2

V. S. Naipaul uses an effective economy in that account of what life is like on a servile newspaper. After a summary in general terms, he confines himself to a handful of graphic examples; and it is all he needs. He picks out a single specimen of the kind of institution Mr Biswas visits as a reporter; three specimens of the kind of thing Mr Biswas sees but cannot report; and two glimpses of Mr Biswas at work, striding the workplaces and hobnobbing with the top man. Those examples no more represent the whole of Mr Biswas's activity than the pictures in a strip cartoon represent everything the characters do. But the part stands for the whole. Indeed, the part works better than a list of the whole would ('he visited orphanages, prisons, asylums . . .'): it is brief, so the reader has no time to be bored, and it is presented in pictures, so the reader's mind apprehends it at once.

It is an important part of the work of writing not just to tell, but to show, your readers what is in your mind's eye. To that end, there are certainly times when a writer is well served by cumulative description. One such time is the moment in chapter 4 of *The Wind in the Willows* (1908) when the Mole and the Rat, lost in the Wild Wood in snow, stumble on the Badger's house and are taken into his fire-lit kitchen. With every detail that Kenneth Grahame piles on—the logs in the hearth, the plates on the dresser, the hams in the rafters—he adds to the reader's sense of contentment. But mostly you haven't the time, or the need. A swift pictorial sample is enough.

Willa Cather, describing in *My Ántonia* (1918) the menace constituted by country girls to the social order of a Nebraska town towards the end of the 19th century, needs only an example or two each time to convey the gentility of the town's life, the dullness of its young men's occupations, the contrasting lack of constraint in one particular country girl's manner, the allure of another: 'The Black Hawk boys looked forward to marrying Black Hawk girls, and living in a brand-new little house with best chairs that must not be sat upon, and hand-painted china that must not be used. But sometimes a young fellow would look up from his ledger, or out through the grating of his father's bank, and let his eyes follow Lena Lingard, as she passed the window with her slow undulating walk, or Tiny Soderball, tripping by in her short skirt and striped stockings.'

Sometimes these vivid instances, standing for a larger whole, are supplied by place-names. In Coward's play *Hay Fever* (1924), Judith Bliss, an actress, says: 'I always longed to leave the brittle glamour of cities and theatres and find rest in some old-world nook. That's why we came to Cookham.' The joke there, besides the internal rhyme, is that Cookham is a dormitory village 27 miles from Paddington. Everything that hearers or readers think they know about life in such a place is evoked for them by a single name.

Place-names can be used for other ends besides comic. Milton brought them out for heroic and sonorous effect. In *Paradise Lost* (1667) he describes Satan's army as more impressive than all the heroes of antiquity, and all King Arthur's knights, 'And all who since, baptized or infidel,/ Jousted in Aspramont, or Montalban,/Damasco, or Marocco, or Trebisond,/Or whom Biserta sent from Afric shore/When Charlemagne with all his peerage fell/By Fontarabbia'—in other words, all the chivalry of the dark ages; named far less comprehensively than that phrase names them, yet far more resonantly.

The master of the vivid instance, as of many other of the techniques of vivid writing, is Macaulay. I quote as evidence a passage from his essay on Frederic the Great (1842). Indeed, I offer this passage as a kind of summary so far, and would point out how many of the virtues I have been pressing are illustrated in it: use of active verbs, punctuation governed by pauses, immediate intelligibility, readiness to repeat words, insouciance about using 'which' in places where pedants want 'that', constructions in parallel, sensitivity to rhythm, exploitation of the way the natural emphasis in a sentence falls at the end, willingness to use commas and semicolons before 'and' in defiance of the Himmlers of the lower fifth, variation in the length of words and sentences, and—in particular—vivid instances, including the evocative use of place-names. The passage (about the mid-18th-century War of the Austrian Succession) is this:

> But the selfish rapacity of the King of Prussia gave the signal to his neighbours. His example quieted their sense of shame. His success led them to underrate the difficulty of dismembering the Austrian monarchy. The whole world sprang to arms. On the head of Frederic is all the blood which was shed in a war which raged during many years and in every quarter of the globe, the blood of the column of Fontenoy, the blood of the mountaineers who were slaughtered at Culloden. The evils produced by his wickedness were felt in lands where the name of Prussia was unknown; and, in order that he might rob a neighbour whom he had promised to defend, black men fought on the coast of Coromandel, and red men scalped each other by the Great Lakes of North America.

Macaulay's prose is direct, unallusive. He deals little in metaphor or quotation (topics we come on to next). But his equipment is as complete as any one writer's can be. The only cardinal virtue not illustrated in the Frederic passage is the virtue of writing as you speak. And it is always possible that Macaulay—whom Sydney Smith called 'a book in breeches'— did actually talk like that, too.

28
FIGURATIVELY SPEAKING

Conditions being as they were at Brinkley Court—I mean to say, the place being loaded down above the Plimsoll mark with aching hearts and standing-room only as regarded tortured souls—I hadn't expected the evening meal to be particularly effervescent. Nor was it. Silent. Sombre. The whole thing more than a bit like Christmas dinner on Devil's Island.

I was glad when it was over.

What with having, on top of her other troubles, to rein herself back from the trough, Aunt Dahlia was a total loss as far as anything in the shape of brilliant badinage was concerned. The fact that he was fifty quid in the red and expecting civilization to take a toss at any moment had caused Uncle Tom, who always looked a bit like a pterodactyl with a secret sorrow, to take on a deeper melancholy.

P. G. Wodehouse, *Right Ho, Jeeves*, Herbert Jenkins, 1934; chapter 8

Besides the picking out of graphic examples, another way to make your subject-matter vivid to your readers is to help them see part of it for a moment in a new way, as if it were something other than it is. That is broadly the job done by figures of speech: metaphor, simile and the rest. A man in whose work it is worth studying them is P. G. Wodehouse. Most of them have classical names, and Wodehouse will have first met them when he was a schoolboy at Dulwich at the end of the 19th century reading Latin and Greek verse; but he bent them gleefully to English prose.

In the queen of these figures, *metaphor*, you write about something as if it actually were something else. Brinkley Court, in our text, becomes a ship with a Plimsoll line, then a theatre with no seats left. (There is nothing against changing your metaphors rapidly; but mix them, taking half the idea from one world and half from another, only for comic effect: 'When we Woosters put our hands to the plough, we do not readily sheathe the sword.')

The single word 'effervescent' is a metaphor: the meal-time conversation is judged as if it were a drink. ('Not particularly effervescent' is a specimen of *litotes* or *meiosis*: understatement. The occasion was likely to be dead flat.) Aunt Dahlia, calculatedly refusing food, reins herself back from the trough: a horsewoman, she is spoken of as if she were a horse. Civilization becomes a rider. Even if your material is abstract, fresh metaphor can still help you make pictures in your reader's mind.

Or you can stop short of saying that something is itself something else and say instead that it is like something else: the evening meal like Christmas dinner on Devil's Island; Uncle Tom like a pterodactyl with a secret sorrow: *simile*. Wodehouse is particularly strong on simile. A cross and hungry Tuppy Glossop looks 'like a wolf on the steppes of Russia which has seen its peasant shin up a high tree'. Madeline Bassett, a soulful girl, produces a sigh that sounds 'like the wind going out of a rubber duck'. (All the examples in this chapter are from the same book.)

You don't have to begin your simile with 'like', as long as a comparison is expressly drawn. Jeeves (egghead valet to Wodehouse's narrator, Bertie Wooster) preserves 'the quiet stolidity of a stuffed moose'. Of a characteristically instantaneous Jeeves exit: 'Many a spectre would have been less slippy.'

You can combine your simile with a play on words: *paronomasia*. '"It is not twenty-four hours since she turned me down." "Turned you down?" "Like a bedspread."' (That last phrase understands 'turned down' in a sudden different sense.)

Or you can further enliven your simile with manifest overstatement: *hyperbole*. After drinking one of Jeeves's post-hangover pick-me-ups, 'the subject is aware of something resembling a steam hammer striking the back of the head'.

You can take an ordinary noun and set it in a fresh light by using a transferred epithet: *hypallage* (four syllables, like hyperbole). 'I wandered out into the garden, smoking a tortured gasper...' '"And yet, Jeeves," I said, twiddling a thoughtful steering-wheel...' The adjectives 'tortured' and 'thoughtful' belong in logic to the subject, 'I'; but they are momentarily shifted.

Or in place of your ordinary noun you can put a related noun conveying the same idea: *metonymy*. The relation may be of shape, for example: Wodehouse uses a whole range of such equivalents for the word 'head'. 'She shook the pumpkin.' 'The lemon had scarcely touched the pillow...'

You can express the whole in terms of the part: *synecdoche*. Unhappy human beings become aching hearts or tortured souls. In a striking reduction, Bertie's cousin Angela becomes 'a simple, jolly, kindly young pimple'. The vivid instance itself, our theme in the chapter before this one, is synecdoche on an enlarged scale. Tuppy, Angela's suitor, is a rugger-player: Wodehouse calls him 'excellent at blocking a punt or walking across an opponent's face in cleated boots'—epitomizing rugger in two glimpses. One Wodehouse refinement of synecdoche is to let part of a worn phrase stand for the whole: Jeeves's face is described as his 'finely chiselled'—the reader supplies 'features'—and later as his 'f-c'. (That could also be classed as

117

aposiopesis, a breaking off or falling silent before the end of a phrase when the reader can infer the rest.)

One other device, not strictly a figure of speech, can also carry the reader's mind to some other thing than the precise matter in hand: *quotation*. Wodehouse makes plentiful use of this, too. Bertie never recognizes Jeeves's quotations, even from verse as familiar as Gray's 'Elegy' ('Melancholy, as I remember Jeeves saying once about Pongo Twistleton when he was trying to knock off smoking, had marked him for her own'); yet Bertie plants a good many in his own narration. 'Something attempted, something done, seemed to me to have earned two-penn'orth of wassail in the smoking-room'; and, that secured, he puts his feet up 'rather like Caesar having one in his tent the day he overcame the Nervii'. In the mind of the reader who remembers the Longfellow poem or the Shakespeare line, sudden ludicrous images blossom of Bertie as village black-smith under the spreading chestnut-tree, or as Julius Caesar in a new cloak in a tent in Gaul.

All of these devices can be sources of illumination and pleasure to your readers. Some of them deserve consideration in a little more detail.

29
WEIGH YOUR METAPHORS

A line . . . circumscribes an area in moral space around an individual. Locke holds that this line is determined by an individual's natural rights, which limit the action of others. Non-Lockeans view other considerations as setting the position and contour of the line. In any case the following question arises: are others forbidden to perform actions that transgress the boundary or encroach upon the circumscribed area, or are they permitted to perform such actions provided that they compensate the person whose boundary has been crossed? Unravelling this question will occupy us for most of this chapter. Let us say that a system forbids an action to a person if it imposes (is geared to impose) some penalty upon him for doing the act.

Robert Nozick, *Anarchy, State, and Utopia*, Basil Blackwell, 1974; chapter 4

The elegance of metaphor is that it can make an idea visible to the mind's eye. Robert Nozick, the Harvard political philosopher, is here considering human rights. (His pitch is that we have fewer than we think we have.) To help us grasp his theme, he uses a metaphor. He talks of our rights as if they were a defined space round us. The metaphor is coherently employed: the defining line round the edge has position, contour; it is a

119

boundary; it can be transgressed (wrongly stepped over), crossed. We are given a picture to hold in our minds as the argument develops.

Metaphor can also entertain. My former editor at the *Sunday Times*, Harold Evans, loved splashes of metaphor to brighten dull leaders—other people's and his own. Metaphor abounds in his book about his editorship of that paper and then *The Times* (*Good Times, Bad Times*, 1983). 'It was the court page which bowled me my first *Times* googly.' A googly, at cricket, is an off-break delivered by the bowler with an apparent leg-break action, or the other way round. Evans could have written '... which gave me my first deceptively awkward question to answer': longer and less graphic. The question itself was whether a woman might call herself 'Ms' instead of 'Miss' in an engagement notice. Difficult, since 'Ms' is hard to say, and therefore hard to read; but Evans decided to allow it, on the faultless ground that, short of fraud, people may call themselves what they like. The second difficulty, the hidden spin on the ball, was that the editor of the court page—whose good will Evans needed to keep—would not disclose her own opinion.

Metaphor is most useful where ideas are most difficult, most abstract. It is rife in the language of religion: the body as something to wear, sin as something to carry, heaven as a harbour. My father, a theologian, explains the subject-matter of his best book thus: 'There are three great biblical metaphors, taken respectively from the battlefield, the altar of sacrifice and the law-court, which seek to describe and explain the action and the passion of the Cross. They are Christ as Victor; Christ as Victim; Christ as Criminal; and they are later expanded into systematic theories of atonement. All three are attempts to express a paradox which is conceptually inexpressible, namely that here something was done for sinful men—not only *by* God but *to* God' (J. S. Whale, *Victor and Victim*, 1960).

Metaphor is nevertheless risky stuff. Because it asserts

120

equivalences, and not just likenesses, it can fuse with reality: telling which is which becomes difficult. (That is one of the great disputes within modern theology.) If I see my life as a lottery, I may well live it recklessly; if I say that I am on a journey through life, 'And nightly pitch my moving tent/A day's march nearer home' (as the metaphor in James Montgomery's 1835 hymn says), I may live purposefully. The peculiar acrimony that can afflict both religion and politics is at least partly explained by the prevalence, in the language of both pursuits, of metaphors from fighting.

For that reason and others, special care is needed in the handling of metaphor, and a special alertness to the occasions when you may be using metaphor without being aware of it. A word's normal meaning can show through. If you say that an MP plays a representative role, you are using a metaphor from the theatre, and you cannot entirely wash your hands of the implication that there is pretence in what the MP does. It is no defence to say that the metaphor is so tired as to be almost lifeless: that is another reason why you do well to think before you use it.

Or the careless use of metaphor may set up a picture that is unintended and distracting. Even the keenest-witted writers sometimes overlook that kind of slip. Michael Dummett, the Oxford philosopher, writes (in *Truth and Other Enigmas*, 1978): 'This sketch of one possible route to an account of why, within mathematics, classical logic must be abandoned in favour of intuitionistic logic obviously leans heavily upon Wittgensteinian ideas about language.' To equate the course of an argument with a route on a sketch-map is fair enough. The awkwardness is in the phrase 'leans heavily': a sketch can lean, but it can lean heavily only if it is on heavy material or in a heavy frame. I doubt if Professor Dummett had that picture in his mind, or wanted to transmit it to his reader's.

The extreme of carelessness is the mixed metaphor. On the

day I draft this chapter, *The Times* reports a Scottish MP as asking in the Commons whether the teething troubles of the advanced passenger train have been ironed out. In the mind of the reader or listener who is paying attention, the image created is first absurd and then horrific. Almost as troublesome is the metaphor followed too far: 'If the train's teething troubles have not been soothed away, will the minister consider the ointment of further research-and-development money, or does he favour the teething-ring of user-trials?' Even if the teething metaphor was an accurate one in the first place (a large assumption, since the metaphor implies that the troubles are sure to disappear in time), each fresh equivalence makes the truth more strained.

In sum, use metaphor deliberately and sparingly. Professor Nozick's main metaphor is deliberate. His metaphors in 'unravelling' and 'geared' are probably not. Sound in themselves, they create fresh pictures too close to the main metaphor and to each other. They would have been better ironed out.

30
A GOOD LIKENESS

He undressed behind a dune and was disappointed to find Mrs Sturgis and Mrs Gates preparing to have a picnic on the stretch of beach where he wanted to swim and sun himself. He was also disappointed that he should have such black looks from the old ladies who were discussing canned goods and the ingratitude of daughters-in-law while the surf spoke in loud voices of wrecks and voyages and the likeness of things; for the dead fish was striped like a cat and the sky was striped like the fish and the conch was whorled like an ear and the beach was ribbed like a dog's mouth and the movables in the surf splintered and crashed like the walls of Jericho . . . Then he began to swim—a sidestroke with his face half in the water, throwing his right arm up like the spar of a windmill—and he was never seen again.

John Cheever, *The Wapshot Chronicle*, Harper & Row, 1957; chapter 36

One thing will often remind you of another thing—especially if you are an old man, like John Cheever's New England patriarch Leander Wapshot, your head full of remembered observations and imaginings (a condition which Cheever's long, little-punctuated sentences suit). Sometimes you will want to share those reminders with your reader, in a simile, expressly pointing out a likeness.

Similes are broadly of two kinds. They can be merely decorative, signalling a moment of common pleasure between the writer and the reader, as one suggests and the other notices a parallel not remarked before. Most of the similes in the Cheever passage are of that sort. Or they can be functional, perceptibly increasing the clarity with which the reader sees the image in the writer's mind. In that group might come the picture of the old man's arm rising and falling in an arc, like the slow-turning sail of a windmill.

In the first, ornamental category belong those lengthy Homeric similes which Matthew Arnold adopted in 'Sohrab and Rustum' (1853). Mortally wounded by his own unknowing father, Sohrab survives through a recognition and reconciliation scene and then pulls the spear out of his body: 'all down his cold white side/The crimson torrent ran, dim now and soiled,/Like the soiled tissue of white violets/Left, freshly gathered, on their native bank,/By children whom their nurses call with haste/Indoors from the sun's eye'. The simile is no real aid to picturing the outflow described: the most that can be said for the violets is that they provide a parallel instance of life pointlessly taken. There is a comparably non-functional flower simile in Disraeli's novel *Coningsby* (1844): '"'Tis but simple fare," said Coningsby, as the maiden uncovered the still hissing bacon and the eggs, that looked like tufts of primroses.' The likeness is far-fetched: the leaves of primroses are nowhere near the colour of the whites of fried eggs, unless the eggs are uneatable; but it raises a smile. And I find an egg simile of the same kind in J. G. Farrell's novel about an Irish hotel after the First World War, *Troubles* (1970): as a result of a storm, 'the servants' wing was uninhabitable: the roof had been taken off as cleanly as the top off a boiled egg.' The sentence says hardly more than '. . . taken clean off' would have done, and anyway many people take the tops off boiled eggs fairly messily. The parallel entertains rather than enlightens.

124

Functional similes are less often encountered than the decorative kind; but they can be found, and sometimes contrive to be entertaining in addition. An example is Lady Wishfort's famous simile as she peers into her mirror in Congreve's *The Way of the World* (1700): 'I look like an old peeled wall.' Her skin, with its blotches and crevices and cavities, seems suddenly brought under a magnifying-glass. Again, in the middle volume—*Dwellers All in Time and Space* (1982)—of Philip Oakes's sharply recollected memoirs, a Sister Beryl at a children's home is almost photographed in simile: 'Her hair was the colour of old bracken and curiously dull, as if the oils had been baked out of it. Her shoulders drooped and her belly protruded like a giant tear-drop which only her dress prevented from rolling to the floor.' In the same category sometimes belong those similes that journalists bring out to make large numbers apprehensible: instead of saying that the American battleship *New Jersey* could fire shells weighing 2000 pounds, a feature article in the *Sunday Times* (about Lebanon, in February 1984) said 'She can fire shells the weight of a Volkswagen'.

Similes, and especially the decorative kind, can nevertheless grow tiresome. Max Beerbohm reminds himself of that truth when he starts on a flower simile in his Oxford novel, *Zuleika Dobson* (1911): 'The moon, like a gardenia in the night's button-hole—but no! why should a writer never be able to mention the moon without likening her to something else—usually something to which she bears not the faintest resemblance? . . . The moon, looking like nothing whatsoever but herself, was engaged in her old and futile endeavour to mark the hours correctly on the sun-dial at the centre of the lawn.' So in fact he abandons a simile for a metaphor (since personification is a form of metaphor); and he is wise. Readers can quickly have enough of simile. The Cheever passage is saved from tedium only because the similes are not so much an exposition of likenesses as an expression of a character's mind. Ordinarily, an excess of similes can convey a sense that a writer is straining after effect, showing off. Simile, therefore, needs even more niggardly use than metaphor.

Metaphor is after all the more subtle form of the two. Every metaphor presupposes a simile, is a development from a simile, is more economical and evocative than the simile would have been. A metaphor is a claim about reality; a simile dare not go so far. Beerbohm's moon is not itself a gardenia, it is only like a gardenia; but it is, for a moment, a persistent and disappointed recorder of time.

31
DOUBTFUL DECORATIONS

The sun continues to shine into the kitchen. Standing by the toaster, Erica contemplates her children, whom she once thought the most beautiful beings on earth. Jeffrey's streaked blond hair hangs tangled and unwashed over his eyes in front and his collar in back; he hunches awkwardly above the table, cramming fried egg into his mouth and chewing noisily. Matilda, who is wearing a peevish expression and an orange tie-dyed jersey which looks as if it had been spat on, is stripping the crusts off her toast with her fingers. Chomp, crunch, scratch.

Alison Lurie, *The War Between the Tates*, Heinemann, 1974; chapter 1

All figures of speech need dispensing with a cautious hand; some with an especially cautious hand.

A case in point is the figure of which the proper name is *syllepsis*, and of which 'wearing a peevish expression and an orange tie-dyed jersey' is an example. In syllepsis, one word governs two other words or phrases, correctly enough, but with a shift in its sense. The word 'wearing' is there first used metaphorically and then understood literally. Substitute 'green skirt' for 'peevish expression', and the syllepsis disappears: the sense in which 'wearing' is understood the second time is then exactly the same as the sense in which it is used the first time.

Writers of advertisements enjoy syllepsis. An American hotel chain uses the slogan: 'Spend a night, not a fortune'. In the first half of that injunction, 'spend' means 'pass'; in the second half it is understood as meaning 'pay out'.

Fowler, in *Modern English Usage* (1926), says that syllepsis is 'so much overdone as to be now a peculiarly exasperating form of worn-out humour'. What may well have been a statement of fact in the 1920s should be read rather as a warning in the 1980s. Syllepsis does not seem to me to be at present overworked in published writing; but if it were, it could indeed become a bore. It is a joke against your readers. After 'wearing a peevish expression and . . .', they expect something like 'a look of distaste': instead they get 'an orange tie-dyed jersey'. You have fooled them. That will amuse them, once; but if you keep doing it, it will certainly exasperate them. Alison Lurie, a neat and witty writer who likes the figure, appears to use it about once a book. (In her 1969 novel *Real People* I find another instance: '. . . to make cinnamon toast in the kitchen after the sitter had gone home, or love on the living-room rug'.) I should have thought that was the right ration: about once every 60,000 words.

The figure is often called *zeugma*; so often as to establish that as a permissible name. But grammarians insist that strictly a zeugma is a usage where the word governing two other words or phrases doesn't quite work, in point of grammar or sense, when it's understood the second time. If Alison Lurie had written 'His hair was tangled and his eyes bleary', that would have been a zeugma. The word 'was' applies to both adjectives; yet, supplied the second time, it gives you 'his eyes was bleary', when you need 'were'. This roughness is easily smoothed by putting in the 'were'; and it is worth smoothing, to keep the good opinion of alert readers.

Another figure of speech that needs watching is *alliteration*, the repetition of the same letter or sound. A single repetition, as with 'the most beautiful beings' in the Lurie passage, is nothing: it can be the random result of looking for the right word (as that alliterative phrase 'random result' was). But if you were to write 'the most beautiful beings ever born', or (since internal as well as initial sounds count) 'indubitably the most beautiful beings', then you would appear—whether or not this was the fact—to have intended the alliteration. And the trouble with alliteration is that it arouses in your readers the suspicion that you have chosen some of your words more for their sound than for their sense.

The fact is that alliteration is almost entirely a device of poetry, where word music is its own justification. Swinburne adored it: 'The mother of months in meadow or plain/Fills the shadows and windy places/With lisp of leaves and ripple of rain' (*Atalanta in Calydon*, 1865). In that third line, the alliteration has a value beyond mere musicality: it simulates the sounds, themselves repetitious, made by young leaves and spring rain. It is a device allied to *onomatopoeia*, the process of devising words (or using words already devised) to express their sense in their sound. 'Chomp' and 'crunch', in the final sentence of the Lurie passage, are two such.

A last figure to beware of is *aposiopesis*, or breaking off short and leaving the reader to finish. It is useful, I suppose, if you're writing dirty verse. There is a poem which I have never seen written down called 'Christmas day in the workhouse'. It contains a quatrain which goes something like this: 'Then up spoke a brave old pauper,/With his face as bold as brass:/"You can keep your Christmas pudding;/You can..."' There aposiopesis serves a purpose of a kind. The figure is much used in ordinary speech to soften sarcasm: 'I always thought people had to go to school looking clean and tidy, but...' The words left out there, for the hearer to supply, are a continuation of the sarcasm: something like 'things may have changed' or 'you

129

know best'. Notice, though, that the gibe would gain in effectiveness if the 'but' part were either completed or (better still) left out altogether. In written work, the device looks even more fumbled.

Three dots, or points, are in general a mark of punctuation you will seldom need. Their best understood use is to mark words left out within a quotation. Rarely, you may need them at the end of a sentence to indicate that you want the pitch of the reader's inner voice kept up, not dropped. Those uses aside, they are best left in the drawer. It seems to me unwise to use them to telegraph a joke or a surprise: 'He opened the door, and there stood ... a policeman.' Any regular reader of French newspapers knows how tiresome that device becomes in French journalistic prose. It would have the same effect if used at all extensively in English. It tries to dictate a response, as the stand-up comedian does with his cry of 'Wait for it' before the punch-word. Readers need subtler handling than that. Build the story well enough, and the policeman will seem suitably surprising without his three dots.

32
AND I QUOTE

But the loudest cheer of the day and a fanfare greeted the bride, prepared by the Emanuels as a bride adorned for her husband in ivory silk taffeta and old lace. According to the heavy folders of heavily embargoed information, her veil was hand-embroidered with 10,000 tiny mother-of-pearl sequins, as they say in *Come Dancing*. Lo where she comes along with portly pace, on her father's arm, in her strong toil of grace, and with her train stretching 25ft down to the bridesmaids and pages.

Philip Howard, 'A grand act in the theatre of kingship', *The Times*, 30 July 1981

The questions about quoting—borrowing other writers' good things—are two: first whether you should do it at all, and second whether you should flag your borrowings with quotation-marks. Philip Howard, in his page-one report on the wedding of the Prince and Princess of Wales, answered yes to the first question and no to the second; rightly, it seems to me.

The uninteresting motive for quoting is the wish to strengthen your arm with someone else's authority or someone else's precision of phrase. You do then need to acknowledge, with names and quotation-marks, what you are up to. That kind of quoting is sometimes helpful, though derivativeness can quickly become a bore.

The interesting motive, which was (I take it) Howard's, is the aim to shed light on one thing by setting beside it the analogous picture of another thing. You can do that with a figure of speech—a simile, a metaphor; you can do it with a quotation, which calls up, in the minds of readers who recognize the quotation's original context, the pictures belonging to that context.

In an article of two dozen paragraphs, Howard quoted a dozen separate literary works published across nearly 400 years. The technique suited a day when times past were much in the air, and it gave Howard's description a changing series of added pictorial backdrops. The paragraph I take as my text was particularly fruity with quotation.

'A bride adorned for her husband' is from Revelation 21:2 (Authorized Version, 1611): the picture is of the new Jerusalem, the heaven-sent prize. 'Lo where she comes along with portly pace' is from Spenser's wedding poem 'Epithalamion' (1595). That was Howard's chief source. He took five different passages from it, and one from its fellow, 'Prothalamion'; evoking, in readers who knew those poems, countless images of the combined solemnity and revelry of great Elizabethan weddings. 'In her strong toil of grace'—*toil* in the sense of *net*— is from Shakespeare's *Antony and Cleopatra* (*c.* 1606): it drew a cunning parallel between the bride's train and the metaphorical net in which Cleopatra caught admirers.

Yet in the whole quotation-encrusted piece, the mildly derisive mention of *Come Dancing* was the nearest Howard came to naming a source. The case for that silence is that a quotation of this kind, intended to evoke analogous pictures, only works for readers who recognize the source straight away; and if they do recognize it, they will be merely irked at having it identified.

What should you do about readers who don't recognize your

quotations, though? First, keep those readers to a minimum by using only such quotations as are likely to be picked up by the bulk of the readers you are writing for. A vicar, writing in his parish magazine about a new smoke-detector that replaces a somnolent verger, may safely say that the church's fire-prevention system rests not now by day or night: most of his readers will have sung the Ellerton hymn from which that line comes. Howard, similarly, writing in *The Times*, could reckon that a fair proportion of his readers would pick up a reasonable number of his references.

For a more general readership, though, the problem is severe. Such common culture as there was in Britain has been dwindling for years, as the sheer volume of things to read and learn has multiplied, as broadcasting has divided into many channels, and as Christian worship has become both less frequented and more diverse than it was. There are not many phrases you can quote with any assurance of having the allusion generally picked up. One of the few things left that almost everybody reads is advertisement hoardings; which is why certain advertising slogans—like the one for the beer that refreshes those parts other beers cannot reach—are more often quoted than their absolute wit warrants.

So, second, leave out the quotation-marks. Then readers whose literary furniture is different from yours need not feel that you are thrusting your quotations under their nose—may not even notice them. Those rare *Times* readers unversed in the book of Revelation, for example, might simply have taken 'a bride adorned for her husband' as a phrase of Howard's own devising.

Hazlitt, whose head so bulged with lines from earlier literature that he could hardly write a page without bringing two or three of them out, begins his 1822 piece on 'The Fight' like this: '*Where there's a will, there's a way.*—I said so to myself, as I walked down Chancery-lane, about half past six o'clock on

133

Monday the 10th of December, to inquire at Jack Randall's where the fight the next day was to be; and I found "the proverb" nothing "musty" in the present instance.' He was remembering how Shakespeare has Hamlet repeat four words of a forgotten saw, break off and say: 'The proverb is something musty.' Those of Hazlitt's readers, in 1822 and later, who recognized the quotation will not have needed it signalled as such; those who did not will have been slowed and irked by the signals. Much better leave them off. A further benefit is that if the shape of your sentence—like Hazlitt's—prevents your using your quotation verbatim, you can change a word here and there without having quotation-marks flashing on and off like stop-lights. You are alluding, not quoting; and the allusion is a private pleasure between you and those of your readers who happen to be able to share it.

33
ON THE RECORD

As they talked, the Americans began to form conclusions about the four men they found themselves principally dealing with. Admiral Anaya struck them as the toughest member of the junta. He told the Americans bluntly that the British fleet was incapable of mounting a successful action 'because it will break down'. The British would rather negotiate than fight, he said, 'because all they are really interested in is oil.' The Argentinians, on the other hand, said Anaya, would fight to the death. 'My son is a helicopter pilot,' he said at one stage. 'The proudest day of my life will be when he lays down his life for the Malvinas'—to which Haig replied quietly, 'You know, when you see the body bags, it's different.'

The *Sunday Times* Insight Team, *The Falklands War*, André Deutsch and Sphere, 1982; chapter 11

Playwrights and novelists are not the only writers who disclose character through dialogue. In that account of a mediating visit to Buenos Aires in April 1982 by Alexander Haig as American secretary of state, contrasting national and personal characters are more economically and effectively caught in scraps of reported dialogue than they could have been in whole paragraphs of exposition. Here we're not dealing with literary quotation but with what journalists call quotes. Literary quotation lifts you into a higher register than you were in before: quotation from ordinary, unstudied speech will often drop you into a lower. The gain is in variety; more than that, humanity. A snatch of quoted speech reminds your reader that these serious things you're writing about do in fact involve human beings; and that you or your informants have listened to them.

The device is especially effective at the end of a paragraph. Often your quote doesn't add new information, and by denying it a separate paragraph you are disclaiming any suggestion that it does; but by presenting the same facts in other phrases you authenticate them and bang them home. Earlier in the same book as our text there is a paragraph which sums up the story of how the original Falklands garrison of 68 marines under Major Mike Norman had succumbed to the Argentinian invasion. 'As a result, Norman discovered that his men had not suffered a single casualty: on the other hand, in the course of firing 6,462 rounds, they had killed five (two confirmed), wounded seventeen (two confirmed), taken three prisoners and knocked out an Amtrac. "We came second," Norman said, "but at least we won the body count."'

Grim, military humour gives the paragraph a sudden edge. It was at the *Sunday Times* that I first learnt about ending the occasional paragraph with a quote; but the trick's usefulness is not merely journalistic. A sales report can be enlivened with a line from a shopkeeper. He will be purveying those precious commodities, variation and the vivid instance.

A few technical matters arise. The mark of punctuation before a quote may be a colon, a comma or nothing at all, according to the length of pause you want. But is there always a capital letter at the beginning, and does the final mark of punctuation go inside or outside the quotation-mark at the end? The way to tell is to think back to the original. Those two quotes beginning 'because' in our text: would they have had a capital B in the original? No: each time, they are the latter half of whatever sentence the admiral spoke; whereas (further down) the Y of 'You know . . .', although it comes in the middle of a sentence in the book, stood at the beginning of Haig's sentence.

The same with punctuation. That this is an uncertain area is shown by the fact that those two identical 'because' clauses are handled differently: in the first one the full stop is outside the question-mark, in the second it's inside. Logic and usage in the abstract suggest that the better course would have been to leave the stop outside both times: the originals, standing by themselves, could not take full stops, because neither of them is a full sentence. On the other hand, the authors may have wanted to indicate that in the first sentence the admiral said more after the five words quoted, whereas in the second sentence he stopped at the word 'oil'. That is in fact the pattern I have followed in this book, where the matter quoted is a full sentence.

The best general precept is that a closing mark of punctuation not properly belonging to the quote goes outside the quotation-mark, and one that does belong goes inside. Look at the last sentence of our text. The admiral's remark—'The proudest day of my life . . .'—will not have ended with that dash after 'Malvinas'; it will have ended with a full stop, not wanted here. So the dash does not belong with the quote, and goes outside. But the full stop that will have ended Haig's reply is wanted, and does belong with the reply; so it goes inside the quotation-mark.

The exception is the comma. I find that most publishers' editors put the comma inside, whether or not it belongs with the quote. The admiral's statement that his son was a helicopter pilot will not have ended with a comma, yet the comma that closes it has crept inside the wire. Purists could defensibly kick it out again. But in the Norman quote, divided into two by the words 'Norman said,' the comma belongs with his words. He

137

did actually say 'We came second, but at least we won the body count.' In that instance, therefore, logic agrees with usage in putting the comma inside.

If all this makes your head spin, and you want a simple rule of thumb to save fuss, put the punctuation-mark inside every time. It will occasionally lead you into difficulties, but only occasionally. ('Why are they shouting "foul?"' They aren't shouting it as a question; very much as a statement.) When that happens, you can allow yourself an exception to your own rule.

Another question concerns single or double quotation-marks. Most newspapers, including the *Sunday Times*, use double, with single for quotes inside quotes. Most publishers, including the publishers of this book, do it the other way round (as in that bracket in the paragraph before this one). When, in chapter 9, I was drawing a distinction between 'Dickens's' and 'Dickens'', it did occur to me for the first time that the newspaper usage might be the better one: a closing single quotation-mark looks just like an apostrophe, and that can confuse the eye. But single quotation-marks are tidy; and the question very seldom matters. As with so many of these doubts, either form will do as long as you stick to it. What you may not do, though many people try to, is use both kinds: double for speech, single for unusual words (if you have to put quotation-marks round unusual words at all). There is no warrant in good usage for that.

34
MAKING AN END

It was on the day, or rather the night, of the 27th of June, 1787, between the hours of eleven and twelve, that I wrote the last lines of the last page, in a summer-house in my garden. After laying down my pen, I took several turns in a *berceau*, or covered walk of acacias, which commands a prospect of the country, the lake, and the mountains. The air was temperate, the sky was serene, the silver orb of the moon was reflected from the waters, and all nature was silent. I will not dissemble the first emotions of joy on the recovery of my freedom, and perhaps the establishment of my fame. But my pride was soon humbled, and a sober melancholy was spread over my mind by the idea that I had taken an everlasting leave of an old and agreeable companion, and that, whatsoever might be the future date of my history, the life of the historian must be short and precarious.

Edward Gibbon, *Memoirs*, *c*. 1797; memoir E

He deserved his moment of joy. When he came to the end of *The Decline and Fall of the Roman Empire*, that summer evening in Lausanne, Gibbon had completed one of the high towers of English prose. The hope of literary fame—that last infirmity of noble mind—was for once justified.

It is a curiously affecting passage; and yet there is one thing in particular about it that intrigues me. Gibbon says nothing about revising. He writes the last lines of the last page, and that's it. There is to be no going back to search out infelicities and inconsistencies. The work is finished. He has taken an everlasting leave of it.

It is true that Gibbon wrote in his head before he wrote with his hand: he says so in that earlier passage from his memoirs quoted in chapter 21. Moreover, he was not always so confident of what he had written: in another passage he discloses that, when he was writing his first volume, he took a long time to find the right tone of voice: 'The style of an author should be the image of his mind, but the choice and command of language is the fruit of exercise; many experiments were made before I could hit the middle tone between a dull chronicle and a rhetorical declamation; three times did I compose the first chapter, and twice the second and third, before I was tolerably satisfied with their effect.'

But now he was on the fourth volume; and at the end of a long and lonely course he was, like many writers since, racing for the line. After our text, he goes on to confirm that the first manuscript of the fourth volume was also the last, and that it went to the printer without any further copy being made—a risk anyway, then as now, given the accidents that can befall a pile of paper. And he adds that, before publication, 'not a sheet has been seen by any human eyes except those of the author and the printer'. (The deadpan implication of the adjective 'human' is that the manuscript has of course been attentively read by the author of all being.)

A second pair of eyes is a doubtful blessing, agreed. Brought to bear in affection, and with the limited aim of pointing out unclarities or places of difficulty, it can be a great help. If it belongs, though, to an editor or sub-editor who doesn't know when to leave well alone, it can do harm. In either case, it cannot absolve you from the duty of seeing that when your words leave you they are in as good shape as you yourself can possibly put them in.

For ordinary writers, if they are adopting a properly professional approach, the moment that Gibbon describes is no more than the ending of the first draft. They know they don't write finished prose first go: they would be frozen by the idea that what first goes down on paper is what will go to the printer. They do the best they can for the moment, in order to use the time and have something to work on. Then they work on it. A walk under the acacias first, by all means, if there are acacias to walk under; but only as a breather before getting back to the desk.

They attend to the sound of each sentence in the head, to its instant intelligibility, to its freedom from avoidable occasions of offence; and for that purpose they consult a dictionary, a style-book, an encyclopaedia. They manipulate word-order, to bring the emphasis where they want it; and sentence-length, to guard against monotony. Here and there they replace a general assertion with a particular instance, or a plain phrase with a metaphorical one. In short, they try to ensure that as far as they can they have kept their readers happy, and written as they would have spoken, and thought in pictures. Then they go through their work again; and, if they are wise, again. If they then type it out themselves, so much the better: typing allows a last, even scrutiny.

That is the important part of coming to an end. Revision can turn poor work into passable, and passable into good.

Devising the actual form of your ending matters less. Endings are not as important as beginnings: if the reader is still with you at the last, you have won anyway. You may need to look back over the main points of your theme (which is in fact what Gibbon's last page does); you may wish to point a moral; you may have anticipated your conclusion at the outset, and need only to drop the last item of evidence or argument into place; you may want to pick up a point or an anecdote you started with.

Since there are many varieties of ending, there is no general advice about endings that can do much for you. Lewis Carroll's is often quoted, as addressed by the King of Hearts to Alice in the trial scene at the end of *Alice's Adventures in Wonderland* (1865): 'Begin at the beginning, and go on till you come to the end: then stop.' The maxim does less for you than it appears to. It still leaves you with the burden of deciding where in your material the proper beginning is, and where the proper end. All it may deliver you from is the temptation to labour your final point. That is something. Once you have identified the last point, the right course is to make it, and make an end.

INDEX OF SOURCES QUOTED

INDEX OF SUBJECTS

146

omissions, but not to signal surprise, 130

emphasis: product of rhythm, 22, 91; derived from colloquialisms, 20, from preceding a punctuated pause, 20, 41, 91–2, 93–4, 113–114, from repetition (pointing up the new matter), 51, 96–8, and from use of long words among short, 100–101, or short words among long, 101–2, or short sentences among long, 105, or short paragraphs among long, 107–8; best not secured by italics, 97

ending: not amenable to advice, 141–2

everybody, *everyone*: at present best treated as singular, 74–5

ex- (former): requirement that whole phrase should be hyphened, 56

exclamation-mark: legitimate after cries or commands, not after indicative sentences, 92–3

factor: to be mistrusted, 29

feature: to be mistrusted, 29

figures of speech: sources of illumination, 115–18, though to be used with caution, 127–30; v. also alliteration, aposiopesis, hypallage, hyperbole, litotes/meiosis, metaphor, metonymy, onomatopoeia, paronomasia, simile, syllepsis, synecdoche, zeugma

full stop: pause for count of four, 31; sentence-separator, 32; allowable before *and*, 33, 93–4; placed before or after end-bracket according to sentence shape, 40

gay: abandoned by circumspect writers, 84

gender: manipulable to clarify reference of pronouns, 52; problematic with pronouns following *anybody*, *everybody*, *somebody*, *nobody*, etc., 74–5, and

with nouns meant to be common, 75–6

genitive: ordinarily formed with plain apostrophe in plural, 36–7, and with apostrophe-s in singular (except for *its*), 38, even after names ending in s, x or z, 35–6

geriatric: to be renounced, 82, 83

gerunds (verbal nouns): to be treated as nouns, 78

greengrocer's plural: a misuse of the apostrophe, 38

hilarious: to be renounced, 82, 84

his: no longer taken as meaning *his or her*, 74

hopefully: to be renounced, 82, 83–4

hypallage (transferred epithet): rare ornament, 117

hyperbole (overstatement): usable ornament, 117

hyphen: sometimes confused with dash, 32; needed for clarity in compound adjectives, 53–4, 55–56, and in compound nouns, 54–55, 62, but not after adverbs, 55; sometimes multiple, 56; sometimes useful as separator, 54

infinitives, split: inadvisable, 79–80

initials: in need of explanation, 47

interpolations: to be punctuated at both ends, 39–41, or at neither, 41, 59; emphasizers of preceding word or phrase, 93

inverted commas: v. quotation-marks

inverted pyramid: possible shape, 16–17

irony: achievable by repetition, 50

italics: to be used reluctantly, except in titles, 97

its, *it's*: different, 38

job-descriptions: best punctuated at both ends or neither, and not used as titles, 59; best used in genderless forms if no gender meant, 75–6

journalists: tempted to write robot prose, 24–5, to use elegant

148

participles and infinitives, 78–80; in some cases imaginary (against punctuation before *and/but*, 5, 33, 93–4, 113–14, against *which* as a substitute for *that*, 63–4, 113–14, against elisions, 70–71, against tail-end prepositions, 70, 71, against *like* for *such as*, 71–2)

semicolon: pause for count of two, 31; under-used sentence-separator, 32; permissible before *and*, 33, 94, 113–14, or *but*, 33, 113–14

sentences: sometimes without verbs, 19–20; emphasized at end, 20, 91–2, 93–4, 113–14; separated by a variety of stops, 32, 33; usefully varied in length, 103–6, 108–10; to be listened to during revision, 141

shapes for a piece: various, 15–18

short paragraphs: source of emphasis, 107–8

short sentences: set off by long, 96, 105

short words: admirable, but not all the time, 47, 99; of Latin as well as Anglo-Saxon origin, 99; foil to long words, 100–101; set off by long words, 101–2

simile: illustration through fancied likeness, 115, 116–17, 123; ornamental, 124, or functional, 125; quickly tiresome, 125–6; less subtle than metaphor, 126

singular and plural: manipulable to clarify reference of pronouns, 52

situation: to be mistrusted, 28

slang: pleasurable but inexact, 20, 25

some: unsafe word, 92

somebody, someone: at present best treated as singular, 74–5

specific instances: v. particular instances

speech: guide to writing, 8, 9, 19–26; enlivening when directly quoted, 135–6

spelling: to be constantly checked for reader's sake, 69

split compound verbs: permissible, 80

split infinitives: inadvisable, 79–80

stress: v. emphasis

structures: various, 15–18

sub-editors: better rendered needless, 140–41

summary: to be made at outset, 13, 14

syllepsis (one word doing two jobs): for rare use, 127–8

synecdoche (part for whole): graphic figure, 117

technical terms: to be explained, 45–8

that: (conjunctive and relative) best left in, 61–2; (relative) freely replaceable by *which*, 63–4, 113–114

theme: illustrated or suggested by material, 9, 12; summed up in a theme sentence, 12, needing careful placing, 16

thinking in pictures: v. pictorial writing

three dots: v. ellipsis

titles: distinct from job-descriptions, 59

transitive verbs: instrument for active writing, 28

typing: best if done by the writer, 141

underlining: to be used reluctantly, except in titles, 97

variation: applicable to word-length, 99–102, 113–14, to sentence-length, 96, 103–6, 113–114, and to paragraph-length, 107–10; worth checking in revision, 141

verbs: best when transitive, 28; splittable when compound, 80

vividness: achieved by graphic examples, 7, 8, 9, 111–14, by writing as you speak, 24, by plainness of phrase, 100, by using place-names, 113, and by using figures of speech, 115–18

Wall Street Journal formula:
possible shape, 16, 17
which: satisfactory substitute for
relative *that*, 62, though not
replaceable by it in non-essential
relative clauses, 62–3, 64, 113–14
word-processors: doubtful aids, 4,
13
words: to be explained if difficult,
47–8, renounced if changing
sense, 82–4, varied in length,
99–102, 113–14, and reordered
to control emphasis, q.v.
writer's block: overcome by

summary-writing, 14, and by
writing as you would speak, 24
writing: teachable in part, 3–4; a
matter of shrewd courtesy, 69
writing as you speak: beneficial, 8,
9, 19–26, 114; to be checked in
revision, 141
written word: improvable, 4;
precious, 5–6, 47

zeugma (one word doing a second
job incorrectly): to be avoided,
128